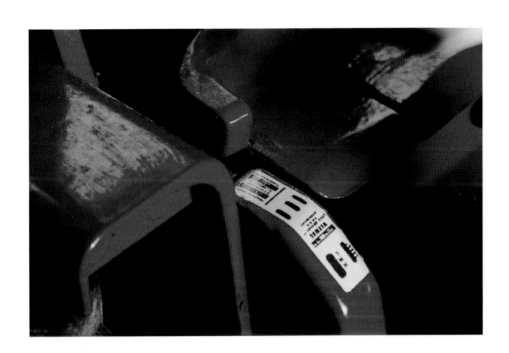

Ertl
Toy Tractors

Patrick Ertel and Catherine Lee Phillips

MBI

For Abby, the best friend a man could ever have.

—*P.E.*

First published in 2004 by MBI, an imprint of MBI Publishing Company, Galtier Plaza, Suite 200, 380 Jackson Street, St. Paul, MN 55101-3885 USA

MBI titles are also available at discounts in bulk quantity for industrial or sales-promotional use. For details write to Special Sales Manager at Motorbooks International Wholesalers & Distributors, Galtier Plaza, Suite 200, 380 Jackson Street, St. Paul, MN 55101-3885 USA.

ISBN 0-7603-2019-5

Acquisition Editor: Dennis Pernu
Editor: Amy Glaser
Designer: Kari Johnston

On the frontispiece: A decal simulated the control quadrant on the right side. The decal is miniscule but so detailed that the word "warning" is legible.

On the title page:
The most popular scales for Ertl toy tractors are, from right to left, 1/28; 1/64; 1/32; 1/43; and 1/16.

On the back cover 1: This Ford 4600 from 1977 is 1/12 scale, but its overall size is small enough that standard 1/16-scale rear wheels are the appropriate size.

On the back cover 2: Allis-Chalmers had no replacement ready for the Landhandler, so it was upgraded somewhat and redesignated the Model 200. It remained in production through 1975.

Printed in China

Contents

Acknowledgments

It is impossible to create a book like this without the cooperation and assistance of others. I would first like to thank my long-suffering staff at *Antique Power* magazine, especially Kathy Pence and Peggy Shank for their forbearance and understanding while I took time from my regular duties to scratch out this text. I also wish to thank Cathy Phillips for directing the photography and Suzanne Ehalt for her assistance with the photography.

Thanks also to all those who shared their knowledge and/or allowed their Ertl toys to be photographed. They are: Robert Zarse, Ray Crilley, L. Neil Pierce, Eldon Trumm, Fred Ertl Jr., Sherry Schaefer, Dennis Long, Kate Bossen, Mary Ertel, and Larry Mayer.

I would also like to thank Annie Reitzler and the staff at the National Farm Toy Museum for their patience and assistance in allowing us to photograph toys in that collection.

Introduction

The story of Ertl farm toys is much more than the story of a successful toy company. It is an American success story, as well as a part of the life stories of thousands of children. From the day Ertl began building sturdy, authentic-looking toy John Deere tractors, the practically indestructible toys became sandbox companions to children who dreamed of someday driving the real thing. As the young rug farmers grew and matured, so did Ertl and its toys. From the first rough, sandcast John Deeres, Ertl progressed into more detailed diecast toys, different makes and scales, and highly detailed scale models. Those youngsters who grew up did not forget their toys or Ertl. As they matured, they preserved the Ertl toys they played with and sought to acquire toys they wished they'd had. The farm toy–collecting hobby developed, and when someone thinks of toy tractors, he or she thinks of Ertl. Although Ertl toy tractors do not bring the highest values on the toy market, they have fueled the farm toy–collector hobby and manufacture authentic-looking toys of tractors. Ertl farm toys have become highly prized collector's items not because of their rarity, but because of the strong feelings of nostalgia they evoke among so many Americans.

This book is an attempt to capture some of those feelings of nostalgia for a more innocent time. It is not a catalog of all Ertl farm toys. Ertl built construction toys, trucks, and pedal tractors at the same time it built farm toys. None of these invoke the depth of feelings that Ertl's farm tractors and implements do, so they are not addressed in this book.

It is important to understand some of the terms used by the toy industry, especially those that have come into common use among toy collectors. A short glossary is included at the rear of the book for your information. Also included is a visual comparison of tractors built to the scales mentioned in the text.

Chapter One

Ertl, Eska, and John Deere

If you are under 60 years old, chances are one of your favorite toys was a 1/16-scale farm tractor built by the Ertl Company. For nearly 60 years "rug farmers" and sandbox ranchers across America have relied on Ertl toy tractors to provide the horsepower to feed their fantasies and spark their imaginations. With the help of Ertl toy tractors, millions of fertile imaginations have tilled thousands of living room acres, dreaming of someday driving a full-size tractor. Other farm toys were available, but Ertl's blend of stamina and realism made Ertl the toy that got the job done. For three generations, when the sandbox had to be plowed, an Ertl tractor plowed it.

The Ertl Company is a classic American success story. Fred Ertl Sr. immigrated to the United States from Germany in the 1920s and settled in Dubuque, Iowa. He made his living as a journeyman gray-iron molder and made cast-iron furnace parts for the Adams Company. Times were hard right after World War II, and Ertl was idled by a strike in 1945. He had a wife and five children to care for and couldn't waste time waiting for a job to open up, so he started his own business.

The contributions of Fred Ertl Sr. and his wife Gertrude to the farm industry are honored in a bronze plaque in the National Farm Toy Museum in Dyersville, Iowa.

(opposite) Fred Ertl's first farm toy was this replica of an Allis-Chalmers WC.

Other manufacturers had made cast-iron toy tractors before World War II, but the demands of the war prevented the manufacture of toys for several years. A burgeoning demand for sturdy toys erupted after the war, and Fred Ertl Sr. proposed to tap into that demand. Another effect of the immediate postwar period was that iron, the traditional material for toy farm tractors, was harder to come by than aluminum. Ertl made his toys from aluminum, which made them light, rustproof, and allowed finer detail. He cast a few cars and trucks, but since he was in Iowa, farm toys were in demand. In 1945 Fred had a pattern made, built casting boxes, dug green molding sand out of a bank, and cast his first toy tractor.

Ertl's first toy tractor was a rough replica of an Allis-Chalmers WC that was painted red. It was cast from aluminum that had been melted in the Ertl family home's furnace in 1945. It was a rather simple and crudely made toy with a cast-in driver and cast aluminum wheels. The front axle was a nail and the rear axle was a steel bolt.

In 1946 Fred produced a more sophisticated toy that was modeled after a John Deere tractor. This model had much finer detail and was a more accurate 1/16 scale than the Allis-Chalmers model. It was a sturdy toy that could withstand rough use,

but it had aluminum wheels that must have made a horrendous sound on a hardwood floor. A toy Farmall with cast-in driver and rubber tires was also produced. The toys were cast in halves in the basement, painted (green for the John Deere and red for the Farmall), then assembled upstairs in the family home. Everyone in the family worked to paint and assemble toys. Neither of the toys carried decals identifying the make of the tractor they were meant to represent, but they were made with such skill and detail there was no mistaking which tractors they were modeled after.

(above) Ertl's first toy tractor resides in a special case in the National Farm Toy Museum.

(right) Ertl's first John Deere toy was a 1938–1946 model and had aluminum wheels .

10

At first marketing was an amateur effort. Fifteen-year-old Fred Ertl Jr. and his brothers took the back seat out of the family car and filled it with toy tractors. They stopped at toy stores and Five-and-Dimes and sold toys right out of the car. The Ertls learned the hard way, but they learned fast. While it got off to a slow start, smart, effective marketing ultimately was at the heart of Ertl's success.

Ertl produced a second John Deere that still had the cast-in driver, but the noisy aluminum wheels were replaced with rubber tires and wheels. The centers of the wheels were painted yellow. It is easily distinguished from later models because the headlights are cast into the sides of the hood near the rear and there is a metal web between the stacks on the hood.

(above) A toy Farmall tractor was produced in 1945, but it was not built in the numbers that the John Deere model was because it didn't have a licensing contract.

(left) This is the second version of the John Deere A diecast by Ertl. It has rubber tires and the headlights are at the rear of the hood.

A third version of the John Deere A, introduced in 1947, had an enclosed flywheel and a steering post that supported the steering shaft. This tractor represented a 1947–1951 model John Deere.

Ertl reached an agreement in 1946 with Bud Essman and Laverne Kascell of the Eska Company to market his John Deere toys to John Deere dealers. This arrangement let Ertl concentrate on what he knew best, casting toys. But these tractors were more than toys. They were used as a promotional tool by dealers, given away to buyers of new tractors, and sold as toys. John Deere wanted to instill brand loyalty in farmers at an early age. If a farmer's first tractor was a John Deere, even if it was just a toy John Deere, he would be more likely to stick with the brand when he had real fields to till.

John Deere had the exclusive right to sell the toys it licensed, which limited sales of the toys to John Deere dealerships, but the project was wildly successful. Soon the growing Ertl family business was moved out of the house and into a small factory building in Dubuque.

John Deere changed its tractors in 1947 and Ertl changed the toys to keep them faithful to the real thing. The flywheel was enclosed, and a steering post with a gearshift quadrant at its base was added. Subtle variations of this tractor are highly prized by collectors. One variant has ribbed front tires, and another has tires that say "Arcade" on the sidewall. Another variation has the words "Ertl" and "Toy" stamped on the sides of the gearshift quadrant.

Ertl built a sandcast model of a Farmall M in the late 1940s. While the body casting is very faithful to the shape of a Farmall M, the wheels were yellow two-piece stamped steel, and it was produced without decals of any kind. Neither Ertl nor Eska had obtained a license to build International Harvester (IH) toys. Because this tractor was not sold under license through International Harvester dealers, it did not sell nearly as well as the John Deere toy. A similar model was later produced by Carter Tru-Scale, and the two are often confused.

This well-preserved original is an example of a 1950 John Deere High Post A.

Although Deere had not changed its real tractors, a new John Deere toy was introduced in 1950. The model number of full-size John Deere tractors was identified by a prominent decal on the hood, but Ertl and John Deere cleverly left the model designation off of the toy. This new toy was a replica of either a Model A or B row crop tractor. Owners were free to decide for themselves whether the tractor replicated and Model A or B tractor. John Deere maintained the practice of not specifically identifying its toy tractors well into the 1980s. This tractor is commonly known as the High Post A because of the height of the post supporting the steering column. Although some collectors believe the size of the toy makes it more similar to a scale model of a John Deere model B, the name High Post A persists.

Both front and rear wheels were two-piece stamped steel with rubber tires. The new toy was the first Ertl John Deere toy to be made without a driver, and it incorporated finer casting detail. It more closely represented the real tractor, making it more valuable to dealers as a promotional tool, and further cemented the relationship between Ertl and John Deere.

This Farmall M from the late 1940s was a second attempt to interest International Harvester in a licensing agreement.

This Ertl John Deere 60 was a Christmas gift to the author in 1955 when he was five years old. A testament to the ruggedness of Ertl toys, it served the three other family "rug farmers" before it was returned to the author in its present condition after 40 years.

In 1952 John Deere introduced a new line of tractors with number designations that replaced the letter designations the company had used for over 30 years. John Deere and Ertl worked closely to choose a model that would represent a typical tractor of the line. The three-plow Model 60 was chosen, and Ertl and Deere engineers worked together to ensure the toy represented the real thing with more detail and real-life features.

The additional detail was the result of a change in manufacturing methods. With production volume increasing every year, Ertl replaced the slow, labor-intensive sandcasting method with diecasting. While diecasting equipment was expensive, the process was faster and allowed more detail to be built into the toy. Ertl tractors soon became the world standard in diecast toys.

The new tractor was a little larger than the High Post A and was the first Ertl toy to have steerable front wheels. Again, though the toy most closely resembles a model 60, no model designation decal was applied, which gave rug farmers the freedom to believe it was "just like Dad's."

Ertl produced its first toy crawler with the John Deere model 40C in 1954. An optional dozer blade could be purchased to turn the tractor into a dozer. This toy's greatest value was as a promotional tool for dealers. Any sandbox farmer can tell you crawlers never function well as toys. The tracks turn hard and need a firm surface on which to operate, limiting the places where they can be played with, and the rubber tracks are fragile and seldom last long.

The Model 60 was made for three years with only one major change. Eska marketed an extensive line of implements built by Carter Tru-Scale to go with Ertl's John Deere toys. Most were pull-behind toys, but a mounted manure loader and a mounted corn picker was later added. The tapered design of the rear axle made mounting the implement difficult. A version came out in 1955 with a modified rear axle that allowed a simplified implement attachment.

John Deere gave Ertl its first major sales account, and Eska solved Ertl's marketing problem by distributing its tractors. Employees had been hired, and a new factory was built in Dubuque on land that left room for expansion. The little company that had started in the basement was poised for growth that would not be long in coming.

Implements for Ertl John Deere tractors helped rug farmers get the job done. Here a High Post A pulls a Model L spreader, and a late Model 60 with a loader cleans up the barn lot.

Chapter Two

Along Comes Farmall

Ertl built its first fully licensed toy for International Harvester in 1955. At the time, International Harvester replaced the venerable Farmall M with a new row crop tractor, the Farmall 400. The new Farmalls had a unique lifting-hitch system that International called the Fast-Hitch. International had high hopes for its invention, and when it wanted an accurate rendering of it included on toy tractors, it turned to Ertl. Ertl created a handsome, realistic toy Farmall 400 for International dealers to sell or give away with a new tractor. The Farmall 400 project was the beginning of a long and profitable association between the two companies.

Ertl Farmall toys were available exclusively at International Harvester dealers. A line of Fast-Hitch implements, including plows and discs, made by Tru-Scale to go with Ertl's Farmall, were also sold at the dealerships.

(opposite top) International's first high-volume Ertl toy was the Farmall 400.

(opposite left) Ertl's Farmall 400 featured International's proprietary Fast-Hitch, just like the original.

(opposite middle) Ertl reproduced the distinctive Farmall front wheel with impressive detail.

(opposite right) The rear wheels on the first Farmall 400s were made in multiple pieces (note the split in the rim). The split rim 400 is a highly desired collector.

Many new Farmall toys were introduced in the last half of the 1950s. When International replaced the Farmall 400 with the Farmall 450 in 1957, Ertl followed with a toy 450. The 450 was similar enough to the 400 that Ertl modified the 400 dies to produce a passable 450. The grille of the 400 with its cast-in detail was smoothed over, and the grille detail was simulated with a decal. A decal with the distinctive white blaze on the side of the hood was added in place of the 400's plain decal, and Ertl had a new model.

International made major changes to its tractors for 1958, both cosmetically and under the hood. An International tractor that was expected to be popular was the new 460, and Ertl modeled it in 1/16 scale. During its production life, the toy 460 came both with and without a Fast Hitch and a belt pulley. It had an improved toy Fast Hitch that was raised and lowered with a lever like the toy John Deere three-point hitch. It looked somewhat less authentic, but it operated much more easily.

(right) Ertl's Farmall 450 was introduced in 1956 with few changes from the previous model.

(below) The introduction of the Farmall 460 forced Ertl to completely redesign its tooling.

(left) Just like the real thing, the Ertl Farmall Fast Hitch could be used like a standard drawbar.

(below) Removing the drawbar attachment allowed the Fast Hitch to be used with mounted equipment.

(left) Eska-marketed implements, such as this Carter Tru-Scale disc, were designed to work with the Fast Hitch.

In 1958 International Harvester introduced its most infamous tractor—the Farmall 560. The toy version proved to be one of Ertl's most venerable toys. Ertl's 560 toy remained in production in one form or another from 1958 until the late 1970s and sold thousands of toys a year. Ironically, although the toy 560 was a resounding success for Ertl, the real tractor suffered disastrous mechanical failures and nearly ruined International Harvester's reputation as a manufacturer of dependable farm tractors.

The first toy 560 was equipped with the same front wheels used on the Farmall 400. While these intricately cast wheels helped make the 400 amazingly authentic for a toy, they didn't resemble the front wheels that were on the real 560 tractor. The 560 also had a working Fast-Hitch, a belt pulley, and a gray rubber muffler. The second series was quite authentic, with all the features of the first series, plus diecast front wheels that more closely modeled the real thing.

(above) One of the later variations of the Farmall 560 toy was this late-1960s version with dual rear wheels. By then the toys came with plastic wheels, compared to the diecast metal wheels that came with the earliest versions.

(right) A version of the Farmall 560 from the 1970s sported a cab. This toy in new–in-the-box condition can be worth up to $1,200.

By 1963, International no longer built the 560, and IH dealers weren't interested in selling the toy 560. Ertl continued to produce the toy for the open market but made little attempt to maintain it as a toy "just like Dad's." Authentic details like the Fast-Hitch and belt pulley were omitted. At least 11 versions were built in all. Various subsequent models deleted features like the muffler, belt pulley, and Fast-Hitch, and replaced metal wheels with plastic in red or white. A version with dual rear wheels and a couple of versions with cabs were also offered. An early 560 with working Fast Hitch and diecast rims is a valuable collectible toy.

Utility-type tractors were a growing part of the market, but they were new to International in 1957. All farm tractor manufacturers were trying to draw attention to their utility tractors in order to lure customers away from Ford, the leader in that market. In the late 1950s, Ertl helped raise the profile of International utility tractors by building Farmall 240s and 340s and International 340 Industrials. The new Internationals were all based on the same casting, with only different paint and decals to distinguish them. All were equipped with a working Fast-Hitch and diecast wheels.

Packaging in the 1950s did little to inspire sales. Ertl tractors were packed in basic two-color boxes like this one.

The Farmall 240 looked identical to this 340 with the exception of the model number decal. An International 340 Industrial was the same as this regular 340, but it was painted industrial yellow and had a heavy-duty industrial radiator grille decal.

When John Deere replaced the Model 60 with the Model 620 in 1956, Ertl followed suit with its toy 620. The real 620 was a significantly improved tractor, but most of the changes were internal, which made it difficult to present the tractor as a truly new model. To distinguish the old from the new model, John Deere applied large yellow decals to the inset in the hood sides. Ertl's task was somewhat easier than John Deere's. No new engineering needed to be done. Ertl simply added a yellow decal to the 60 and a new 620 toy was born.

One of the features that distinguished the real 620 from its predecessor was its three-point hitch. After years of following the industry in hitch technology, Deere finally added an industry standard three-point with draft control in 1956. The hitch was an important new feature, and John Deere wanted to make its availability widely known. Ertl was challenged with the task of developing a working three-point hitch that was realistic and strong enough to stand up to hard play. Ertl rose to the challenge, and soon a second series of 620 toys with a sturdy, working three-point hitch was in John Deere–dealer showrooms. The hitch, which allowed rug farmers to attach implements to their toy tractors just like Dad did to his real tractor, added a new dimension to play and helped Deere promote its new hitch. In an early effort to use toys as a corporate management tool, a few Model 620s were gold-plated and awarded to dealers as a reward for outstanding sales achievements.

(above) A small number of Ertl's John Deere 620s were gold-plated and awarded to dealers who excelled at selling John Deere products.

(far left) The second series Model 620s were equipped with a working three-point hitch.

(left) Once attached, a plow could be raised or lowered by moving a lever next to the seat, just like the real thing.

John Deere introduced another new series of tractors in 1958. Modeling these new tractors would not be as easy for Ertl as modeling the 620 had been. The rounded hood and prominent fenders of the new 30 series were very distinctive. Completely new tooling would have to be designed in order to build toys that represented the new tractors. For all their external differences, the real tractors wore much the same as the older 20 series tractors under the hood, a fact that was little consolation to the pattern makers at Ertl.

Again, Ertl and Deere chose to create a nonspecific model of a row crop tractor. Sandbox farmers agree it is of a size that could allow it to be considered either a 630 or 730, depending on the horsepower needs of the junior farmer.

The new toy tractors introduced a feature that would be part of the John Deere toy line for years to come—diecast wheels. The new wheels were more realistic than the old steel wheels and could be made in-house by Ertl. Originally modeled after John Deere wheels, these diecast wheels found their way onto Oliver and Cockshutt toys before they were supplanted by plastic wheels in the 1960s.

Fenders were standard equipment on John Deere's 30 series tractors and were included on Ertl's toy version. The fenders were attached with screws, and they could be removed to make way for a mounted loader or corn picker. By introducing a toy that a child could work on with real tools, Ertl added yet another level of realism and play value. The same three-point hitch used on the 620 was also used on the 630 for another realistic play feature. A rubber muffler was used that increased the safety of the toy.

The Model 40C crawler also received an upgrade to the Model 420C in 1956. As with the 620, the 420C was re-engineered by putting a new yellow decal on the hood.

Also in 1958, Ertl introduced a model 430U utility tractor. This was John Deere's first utility tractor and represented an opportunity for both Ertl and Deere. For Ertl it was a chance to build a lighter, less complex, and less expensive toy, and for Deere it was a promotional opportunity for its new style of tractor. The 430U was initially built with a three-point hitch, but although existing implements would fit, they were not an authentic size. Even a child knew a little John Deere 430 couldn't pull a four-bottom plow, so the three-point was soon dropped. Plowing the living room rug took a lot of horsepower, and little utility tractors weren't especially popular with junior farmers. Their scarcity makes 430s especially prized by today's collectors.

Ertl's John Deere 630 had removable fenders, a working three-point hitch, and accommodated a variety of mounted implements. It retailed for a little over $2.

By the mid-1950s the belief that "newer is better" that had pervaded the automobile industry had taken hold in the farm tractor industry, too. Tractor manufacturers had previously changed the look of their tractors every decade or so. Now they changed their tractors every two years in an effort to make them seem newer and better. Every time an original equipment manufacturer (OEM) company changed the look of its tractors, Ertl had to redesign and retool its toys. For every new toy, Ertl and OEM designers worked together to create accurate scale models, and then dies had to be machined based on these models. This was an expensive process that required many hours of work by skilled craftsmen. The cost of this development work was built into the price of every toy. Obviously the price of a toy that would only be on the market two years before it became obsolete could be lowered if it could be kept in production after the OEM replaced it with a newer model.

With Ertl's model 430U John Deere utility tractor, John Deere had toys to match its two biggest-selling tractor lines, row crops and utilities.

Ertl reached an agreement with International and John Deere that allowed the company to create toy tractors using John Deere bodies and Farmall wheels. These toys were sold on the open market and helped absorb the cost of tooling for new models.

The toy line had grown from a single model of a John Deere tractor to two John Deere models and four Farmalls. On the surface that's not an impressive increase in the model line, but Ertl had worked hard to achieve it. By mirroring the model changes of its two OEM licensees, Ertl had tooled up for and built four toys that had rapidly become obsolete and were no longer in production. A line of products that could be counted on two hands would not sustain a company forever. The Ertl Company was at a point in its business life where it needed to grow or it would vanish. Not surprisingly, Ertl chose to grow. The next decade put the company on a path to become the world's premier farm toy manufacturer.

In the late 1950s Ertl produced a generic tractor for toy stores. It was assembled with a John Deere body and Farmall wheels.

Chapter Three

Ertl on Its Own

Ertl and Eska ended their relationship in 1959, leaving Ertl with the challenge of making and marketing its toys. Ertl immediately set out to cut costs, expand the market for its toys, and expand its product line. With the agreement with Eska behind them, Ertl was free to pursue its own licenses with the OEMs. Fred Ertl Jr. immediately went to work to bring all the major OEMs into the Ertl fold.

Ertl could increase profit margins if it could extend the life of its tooling beyond two years, but OEMs wanted their latest tractors, not last year's model, cast in toys. In the early 1960s, Ertl began selling toys directly to general toy retailers once they became obsolete in the dealerships. John Deere, International, and other OEM dealers still had exclusive rights to new toys that modeled their current tractors, but instead of scrapping the dies for obsolete tractors, such as the Farmall 560 and John Deere 630, Ertl continued to sell them on the open toy market. More markets and lower costs meant a better chance at survival in the increasingly competitive toy industry.

Ertl entered the 1960s with three OEM licenses: Caterpillar, International, and John Deere, but that didn't last for long. By 1960 Allis-Chalmers was on board and more licenses were in the works. With more dealers to sell to, more toys would be sold, but new products meant additional development and tooling costs. It was a vicious cycle.

Clockwise from the front are Series I, Series II, and Series III Allis-Chalmers D-17s. A version of Series III was produced without an air cleaner on the hood and was called Series IV.

The first new toy for Allis-Chalmers was a diecast model of its D-17. The real tractor was available in tricycle, single front wheel, wheatland, and adjustable wide-front axle configurations. Ertl and Allis-Chalmers decided to model the adjustable wide-front version. Ertl's D-17 remained in the line for four years and evolved through four series that roughly mirrored the full-size Series I, II, III, and IV D-17. The first series D-17 modeled the real Series I with its black grille and orange wheels. When Allis-Chalmers introduced its Series II tractor in 1960, it didn't change it much mechanically, but Allis-Chalmers made significant changes in its looks. The Series II had a lighter shade of orange paint that Allis-Chalmers called Persian Orange No. 2, a cream grille, cream wheels, and a larger hood decal without a black border. Ertl's model followed in 1961 and mirrored the changes in the real tractor. Allis-Chalmers introduced a Series III in 1962 and a Series IV in 1964. Their looks were similar with long side decals and a somewhat different beige grille, and the headlights moved from the hood to the fenders. Although the real Series III came out in 1962, Ertl didn't make the changes until 1964. The Series III toy was the same as the old Series II except for the larger hood decal and the new position of the lights. That same year Ertl introduced a Series IV, which was identical to the previous series except that it had no air cleaner on the hood.

The Allis-Chalmers line was completely changed in 1965. Big tractors with squared hoods, known as the hundred series, replaced the old tractors with rounded hoods. Ertl's toy offering, based on the Model 190, first appeared in 1965. The 190 progressed through several series. As the model evolved, so did Ertl's replica. The earliest version had fenders with a sloping panel in front of the tire. In 1969, it was replaced with a version with flat-topped fenders. Until 1972, Ertl's Allis-Chalmers toys were limited to a lawn and garden tractor and updated versions of the 190.

In 1966 Ertl produced its first toy self-propelled combine. Allis-Chalmers, owner of the Gleaner brand, had Ertl build a version of its Gleaner model CII. For 20 years Ertl's toys had been made in 1/16 scale, but because of the real combine's size, the Gleaner was modeled in 1/32 scale. A 1/16-scale toy self-propelled combine would be too large for many playrooms and would weigh 12 pounds or more. The 1/32 scale is a size that is large enough to allow for good detail and small enough that a child can play with it. The Gleaner marked a move into modeling larger machines and began a search for an appropriate scale for the larger machines that were being introduced by the OEMs. In 1969 Ertl produced a toy version of John Deere's 6600 self-propelled combine in 1/20 scale. Ertl later made combines in 1/50, 1/80, and 1/64 scale.

(above) The flat-topped fenders identify the tractor in the rear as an Allis-Chalmers 190 XT, which was released in 1969. The Model 200 in the foreground replaced the 190 XT in 1972. These toys retailed for about $4 when new.

(right) The 1/32-scale Gleaner model F was Ertl's first self-propelled combine.

(above) Ertl produced a model 1030 by putting a 1030 decal on the 930. After a short time, Ertl replaced the round fenders of the 930 with squared fenders like those used on the real 1030.

(left) The Case 930 Comfort King appeared in dealers' showrooms in 1962, and the first Ertl 930 Case model was introduced in 1963. It was the first Ertl toy produced with a separate hood casting.

When the Case 930 Comfort King appeared in dealers' showrooms in 1962, Case had something new to offer farmers—the Comfort King chassis. Ertl was there in 1963 with a model of its first Case toy, the 930 Comfort King. With its seat moved forward and the fuel tank mounted behind the driver, the Comfort King was a significant change in tractor design, and Ertl helped promote the new concept with its toy. This toy was also a significant change for Ertl. Previous toys had been made of two major castings, the body halves. The 930 had two body halves plus a separate casting for the hood. Painting a toy cast in two parts would have required masking the body to paint the Sunset Yellow hood. With its production processes, Ertl found it easier to cast and paint a separate hood and assemble it to the painted chassis.

In 1966 Case married its big 102-horsepower engine to the 930 chassis and essentially built a new tractor with parts that it already had on the shelf. The new tractor was called the 1030. Case soon learned it should have done some re-engineering, as under severe conditions, the 930 transmission proved unable to handle the additional power. In an interesting, though probably not intentional, example of the toy emulating the real machine, Ertl also built a model of the 1030 with parts it had on hand when it should have done some re-engineering of its own. Ertl created its 1030 by putting a 1030 decal on the 930 toy. Unfortunately one obvious new feature of the 1030 was its distinctive flat-topped fenders that replaced the round fenders of the 930. The round fenders on its 1030 were a glaring oversight, and after a short time, probably until the stock was used up, Ertl replaced the round 930 fenders with flat-top fenders. Although this occurred long before the toy-collector phenomenon developed, Ertl accidentally created a collectible toy. Today the round-fendered 1030s are one of the toys most sought after by collectors.

These are three of the many International 404 variants (clockwise from the lower right). The wide-front tractor with three-point hitch and white metal wheels was introduced in dealerships in 1961. The narrow-front tractor with white plastic wheels and the narrow-front toy with diecast rear wheels and plastic front wheels were released in 1961.

The first new International Harvester toy since the 560 was the Model 404. The full-size 404 came on the market in 1961 as a utility tractor and a row crop. The first Ertl toy represented the utility version. International scrapped the Fast-Hitch and adopted the industry standard three-point hitch by then, and when Ertl's 404 showed up in International dealerships, it included a working three-point hitch. In 1964 it appeared as a narrow-front Farmall toy and also as a generic toy with the name "Ertl Toy" on the hood. The real 404 was not a particularly popular tractor, and fewer than 3,000 were built before it went out of production in 1967. The toy outlasted the real thing and remained in the Ertl catalog as a stand-alone toy through 1968 and was sold as part of a truck-and-tractor set in 1969. The model 404 sold new for $2. All versions of the 404 are prized by collectors.

When International replaced the ill-fated Farmall 560 with the Farmall 806 in 1963, the 560 went on to be a workhorse for Ertl for many years. Stripped of its Fast-Hitch, it was sold as a lower-priced toy until 1967 when a version with dual wheels came out. A version with a cab was offered in 1968, and it was available in more configurations in the 1970s.

The Farmall 806 was announced amid great fanfare in 1963. International promoted it as "The world's most powerful tricycle tractor" and enlisted Ertl's help to present the new tractor to the market. Ertl's toy 806 was introduced in 1964 in tricycle configuration. It had steerable front wheels, but it did not include a functioning three-point hitch. The 806 toy remained in production through 1967. The 806 was the basis for a crude wagon-steered Farmall 1206 Turbo that was introduced in 1966.

Farmall toys of the 1960s and early 1970s are so popular that many models have been reissued. This Farmall 806 was built in 1997.

Ertl first made a diecast manure spreader in 1963. It was available in two versions: as a generic toy painted green and an International spreader. The working single beater was spring-driven. The toy evolved over the years. The beater drive changed to a rubber band and chain, and diecast wheels were eventually replaced by plastic. The toy was in the line for many years.

International introduced the first practical farm tractor with hydrostatic drive in 1967. The 656 was a revolutionary tractor, but International did not take advantage of Ertl toys as a promotional tool. An Ertl 656 was unveiled in 1967, but its appeal was that it was a low-priced toy, not a model of the most revolutionary new tractor in nearly a decade. The Ertl 656 was modeled in1/32 scale and had a nonsteerable front axle. It was half the size of the 1/16-scale models and significantly less detailed. While tooling costs for a 1/32 tractor are similar, material costs are lower, so the price could be lower. Ertl marketed the 656 as the "only low priced tractor with brand name identification." It was made of diecast zinc with rubber tires. It was also offered as part of a line of "mini toys" that included a wagon, spreader, disc, planter, plow, harrow, and mower in 1/32 scale. A farm set was available that included the 656, a spreader, a disc, and a wagon.

On August 30, 1960, John Deere stunned the industry with the introduction of its New Generation tractors. John Deere had completely rethought the farm tractor and introduced four new machines—the 1010, 2010, 3010, and 4010—which set the new standard for farm tractors. John Deere went to extraordinary lengths to keep the news of its radical new tractors a secret. Ertl had no model of the new tractors ready for 1960. That didn't last long, as John Deere and Ertl went to work immediately to create a toy to complement the new tractors. The four-cylinder 3010 and six-cylinder 4010 were expected to be the most popular models, so it was logical to base the toy on one of them. The gasoline-powered 3010 was chosen, and by 1961, a model of the new John Deere was available. Two versions of the Ertl 3010 were built, one with a three-point hitch and one without.

(above) John Deere's 3010 was created as a toy in 1961.

(left) This Ertl version of John Deere's 24T baler with bale ejector came out in 1966. The hitch was adjustable from the baling position to transport position, the pickup could be raised and lowered, and a rear hitch allowed it to pull a hay wagon. It came with four plastic hay bales the ejector would throw into the hay wagon.

(above) The 3020 was built in one basic version, but there were many subtle changes throughout its nearly 10 years.

(right) Ertl didn't offer a wide range of John Deere tractor toys, but it produced a wide variety of implements. This Model 994 planter was a popular toy.

John Deere replaced the 3010 with the improved 3020 in 1964. Although the tractors were visually similar and the old 3010 could have easily continued with no changes, Ertl created a whole new toy. The first 3020 of 1964 began a long line of subtle variations on the same theme. In 1964 alone, nine versions of the tractor were built. The major distinctions were toys having either plastic or metal wheels, a version with plastic on the front and diecast metal on the rear, a working three-point hitch, and a wide front-axle configuration. The 3020 was a very popular toy and remained in production through the end of the decade.

Rug farmers of the 1960s had only a few John Deere tractor models to choose from. Some industrial versions of the 440 and 1010 crawlers were available, but agricultural John Deere tractors were limited to the obsolete 630 and 430, which were available at toy stores, and the 3010 and 3020 that were available exclusively at John Deere dealers. Deere's best-selling tractor was the six-cylinder 4020, and it seems logical that John Deere would have had Ertl make a toy replica of it, but it was not to be.

Deere & Company entered the garden-tractor market in 1963 with the introduction of the Model 110 lawn and garden tractor. The "Weekend Freedom Machine" was well suited as a secondary tractor for rural landowners and as a primary tractor for the suburban lawn farmer. Styling that was consistent with the contemporary full-size tractors helped identify the little tractor as a real John Deere.

Ertl's first venture into vintage toys came in 1967 when it offered a 1/64-scale John Deere historical set. This package of seven vintage farm toys was the first of a popular series for John Deere and Ertl. Many different versions of this historical set were available over the years. They were so popular that new series were still released into the 1990s.

(above) Ertl's first 1/64-scale John Deere Historical set was released in 1967. It included a Froelich tractor, Waterloo Boy, D, A, 60, 730, and 4010. Many different versions of this historical set were available over the years.

(left) The John Deere 110 is a tiny toy at barely three inches long, but it is sturdy and nicely detailed.

(above) This mower, painted in John Deere colors, was a generic toy that was also painted red and sold as an International.

(right) Three eras of Ertl toys are represented in this photo. The diecast transport disc is from the 1950s, the four-bottom plow was built in the mid-1960s, and the 4010 tractor was built in the 1990s.

It took more than just a tractor to till a living room. With few exceptions, the few toy implements available in the 1950s were made by Carter and marketed along with Ertl tractors at the tractor dealerships. Ertl changed all that in the 1960s. Although there was a scant variety of John Deere tractors available in the 1960s, rug farmers had many new John Deere implements to attach to their tractors. The John Deere dealer had Ertl-built corn planters, discs, plows, wagons, manure spreaders, and more to fill a young-ster's machine shed. Ertl made a smaller variety of implements for International and Oliver. Some implements, like mowers and discs, were the same toy with different paint and decals. A generic gravity wagon first appeared in 1968. Labor-saving gravity wagons were popular on farms, and Ertl's toy was popular in America's living rooms. The chute on the toy opened by turning a crank wheel, just like the real thing. The first wagons came in IH red, but generic versions in many colors were eventually offered.

(left) Generic gravity wagons remained in the line for years and were branded with a wide variety of names.

(below) Ertl made a 1/16-scale toy of John Deere's Chuck Wagon, a self-unloading forage wagon, beginning in 1964.

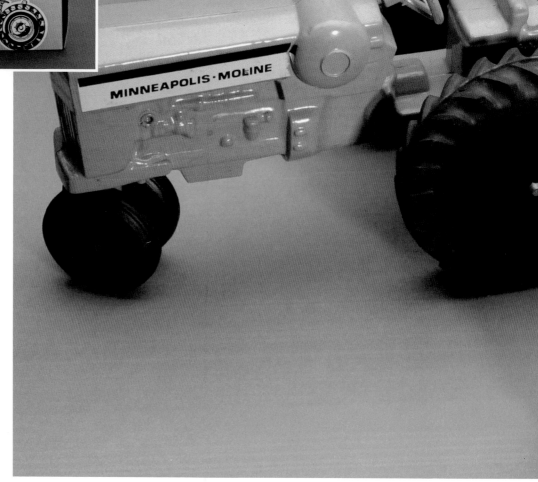

(above) Ertl's first Minneapolis-Moline toy was this 1/25-scale M-602 that was introduced in 1963.

(right) Ertl produced six versions of the 1/25-scale Minneapolis-Moline. Shown here (clockwise from the front) are the gasoline version of the original 1963 M-602, the steerable M-670, the Thermogas special, and the LP version of the original M-602. Also available, but not shown, are the all-yellow gasoline and LP M-602s.

The first Minneapolis-Moline toy produced by Ertl was an inexpensive model of the Minneapolis-Moline M-602 that was introduced in 1963. Ironically, while Minneapolis-Moline promoted itself as "the big tractor experts," its toy was only 1/25 scale, which was about a third smaller than Ertl's standard 1/16-scale toys. The Minneapolis-Moline toys retailed for only $1, while Ertl's 1/16-scale toys sold for $3 to $3.50. The M-602 was nonsteerable and had black plastic wheels. Initially it was painted yellow with a bronze engine and chassis, just like the real tractor. An all-yellow version was released in 1965. The body was cast in both gasoline and LP versions.

In one of Ertl's first instances of custom imprinting, an LP version was produced that carried the "Thermogas" name and was sold through Thermogas dealers. Thermogas was a large LP gas supplier that operated mostly in the upper Midwest. Minneapolis-Moline was a particularly good choice for this program, as the company had always been a leader in producing LP-powered farm tractors. In 1967 Ertl introduced a steerable version they called the Minneapolis-Moline Junior tractor. This model simulated the Minneapolis-Moline M-670. The toy also had black rubber wheels and came only in an LP version. It remained in the Ertl catalog through 1971.

Ertl made only one Massey-Ferguson agricultural tractor during the 1960s. The model 175 was introduced in 1965, and the casting was used for several subsequent toys.

Ertl added another brand to its line in the mid-1960s—Massey-Ferguson. Massey-Ferguson had become a powerhouse in the tractor industry, and in 1965, had Ertl make a toy of its popular Model 175. The 175 was produced in several minor variations. Some have plastic wheels and some have diecast wheels. Some have no front weight bracket, or the bracket may be painted red or silver. In 1967 Ertl introduced a toy of the industrial Model 3165, which was based on the 175. It had a permanently mounted loader and was painted yellow.

In 1963 Ertl introduced the first of many Oliver toy tractors. Toy Olivers had been built by Arcade, Hubley, Slik, and other manufacturers since the 1930s. In the 1950s Slik built Oliver toys in several models that were popular at the dealerships. Ertl's first Oliver toy was a model 1800 row crop and was released in 1963.

Oliver introduced the 1800 in 1960; built the 1800 Series A in 1960, 1961, and into 1962; the Series B in 1962 and 1963; and Series C in 1963 and 1964. Fortunately for Ertl, the differences in these versions were slight and toys of each version could be made by changing decals. The Series A is identified by a long green-and-white checkerboard decal that extends down the side of the hood and has a red Oliver keystone near the rear. The Series B has a long green-and-white checkerboard decal with no keystone. The Series C has a shorter decal with "1800" and "Oliver" in large block type. The Oliver 1800 is a solid, high-quality toy with good detail, diecast wheels, and diecast fenders attached to the axles with screws. It 1965 it was included in a deluxe farm-toy set with a plow, disc, spreader, and wagon, and as a basic set with a wagon and loader.

As tractors became more powerful, putting all the power to the ground became a serious problem. Dual rear wheels and mechanical with front-wheel drive (MFWD) or hydraulic front-wheel assist (FWA) were hot topics in the early 1960s. Oliver produced a FWA 1800 in 1962, and to keep its new tractor front and center before farmers, asked Ertl to produce a toy. The result was the Oliver 1800 FWA, released in 1963. It was the same as the 1800 Series C row crop with the addition of a wagon-steered front axle and chevron-treaded front tires.

In late 1964 Oliver updated the 1800 with the 1850. Although this tractor had 10 percent more horsepower and offered many new features, it looked nearly identical to the 1800. Ertl produced an Oliver 1855 in 1965. It was essentially the same toy as the 1800 Series C with different decals. Later versions omitted the fenders and replaced the diecast wheels with plastic wheels. The 1855 replaced the 1800 in Ertl's Oliver farm-toy sets in 1966.

(above) The long checkerboard decal without a keystone at the rear identifies this as an Oliver 1800 Series B toy.

(left) The Oliver 1800 FWA was the same as the 1800 row crop with the addition of a wagon-steered front axle and front tires with power tread.

Ertl realized that the packaging of its toys was an important part of their appeal in the store, so it constantly improved its effectiveness. From plain, two-color boxes with a simple description of the contents used in the 1950s, the packages evolved into multicolored boxes with sell copy printed on all sides. Realizing that a quality product is its own best advertising, Ertl developed open boxes that allowed the buyer to see the actual toy. Ertl introduced a clever package in 1966 that protected and displayed the toy and also added value. Ford, Oliver, and Farmall farm sets were offered in boxes that unfolded into machine sheds for the equipment.

White Motors purchased the Oliver Corporation in1960 and Cockshutt Farm Equipment Limited in 1962. Some models of Oliver and Cockshutt tractors competed in the same markets. In order to avoid duplication, the Cockshutt line was dropped and Cockshutt dealers were provided with Oliver-built tractors painted in Cockshutt colors. This made it simple for Oliver and Ertl to produce Cockshutt versions of the Oliver tractors already in production. The only requirements were different paint and decals. For 1962 through 1964, Cockshutt's tan-over-red color scheme was used. In 1965 an all-red paint scheme was adopted. Cockshutt tractors were dropped from the Ertl catalog in 1967.

The decade of the 1960s was a time of unprecedented growth for Ertl. The company entered the decade with a few OEM contracts and in 1962 had a catalog that listed six items. In a few short years, the list of OEM licenses had grown to nearly a dozen, and the catalog contained over six dozen items. Marketing, which had mainly consisted of putting plain-looking boxes of toys on OEM dealer shelves, had become as clever and creative as any in the business. Many toys appeared in the catalog multiple times and were packaged in different ways to appeal to different buyers. When the arrangement with Eska ended, Ertl's entire product line consisted of farm toys and a few construction toys. Pedal tractors were added in 1964, and a big line of International trucks swelled the catalog in 1966.

Here are three versions of the same toy. The early Cockshutt 1855 is tan and red, the later 1855 is all red, and the Oliver 1855 is in Oliver green and Clover white.

Chapter Four

New Ownership, Same Vision

With Fred Ertl Sr. near retirement age, the family sold the company to Victor Comptometer, a business-machine manufacturer, in 1967. Fred Ertl Jr. became company president under Victor and continued to lead the company until his retirement in 1992. Under Victor, Ertl continued to grow and added products and innovative marketing methods.

By 1970, Ertl's catalog had grown to 24 pages and contained nearly 100 toys, including farm tractors, implements, trucks, pedal tractors, and farm-toy sets. Selling the toys to farm equipment dealers was still the core of the business, but sales were expanding into towns and cities. The company expanded into the European market in 1974. Ertl worked hard to become more than a toy manufacturer. Its catalog was filled with sales advice for retailers, and Ertl provided creative packaging and displays that were designed to increase sales for nonfarm retailers.

Ertl gave credit for its expanding market to children and said, "Children are children wherever they are and have an instinct for discovering toys that give real play-fun." The company envisioned itself as being in the "child growth business." Recognizing the character-building value of toys that are child-size copies of real things, Ertl continued to build toys that represented the real thing as accurately as cost, safety, and durability allowed.

To maintain authenticity in features and scale, Ertl started with blueprints of the real thing that were provided by the OEM manufacturer. Although the concept had been a hallmark of Ertl philosophy since 1945, Ertl made it official and coined the phrase "Blueprint Replica" and began using it in advertising in 1969. In 1972, the phrase was trademarked and continued to guide the company through the next decades.

Sales of farm toys had been a successful promotional tool for Allis-Chalmers, and the company continued to expand its toy offerings in the new decade. The first new Allis-Chalmers that was introduced in the 1970s was an upgrade of the 190. A version of the Allis-Chalmers 190 had been in the Ertl line since 1965. The 190 evolved through three series with few changes until 1971 when the popular 190 XT Series III Landhandler was released. With the addition of a Roll Over Protection System (ROPS) canopy, bigger tires, and extensive decals, the Landhandler introduced an unprecedented level of detail and features. This attention to detail made the Landhandler one of the first toy tractors to attract the attention of collectors.

The Allis-Chalmers 190XT Series III Landhandler was one of the first tractors to attract the attention of collectors.

The Landhandler had extensive decals to replicate small details.

It was tiny, but Ertl and Allis-Chalmers felt a decal with the word "Landhandler" was an important detail to include.

A decal simulated the control quadrant on the right side. The decal is miniscule but so detailed that the word "warning" is legible.

The radiator grille and A-C logo were simulated with a decal.

Allis-Chalmers introduced a totally new line of tractors in 1973. The new tractors received a radically new look and different color scheme. The new line was called the 7000 series and initially included two models, the 7030 and the 7050, both of which were re-created as toys by Ertl. Changes came fast, and by late 1974, the 7030 was replaced by the more powerful 7040. Ertl's versions of the updated tractors soon followed and required no more engineering than a decal change. When Ertl replicated the 7060, the 7050's replacement, it eliminated the air-cleaner stack.

Allis-Chalmers had no replacement ready for the Landhandler, so it was upgraded somewhat and redesignated the Model 200. It remained in production through 1975.

(above) Ertl released the A-C 7050 in 1973. The similar 7030 was introduced a year later. The new A-Cs were painted a darker orange with a maroon body.

(right) When A-C upgraded the 7050 to the 7060, Ertl followed suit and eliminated the 7050's air-cleaner stack and changed the decal.

Allis-Chalmers changed the paint scheme on its tractors again in 1977 by replacing the maroon chassis color with glossy black and made the model designation on the decal larger. All the Ertl toys received the same new treatment. Ertl made a toy version of Allis-Chalmers' 180-horsepower 7080 in 1979.

The 7045, released in 1978, was the first 1/64-scale Allis-Chalmers. Several variations include a rare version with a large rectangular front decal.

(above) The Case 1070 Agri King was the first of the new Agri King series and served as the basis for many Ertl toys.

(right) The Case Black Knight Demonstrator is one of the most highly sought after Ertl toys.

Ertl's third Case toy was produced in 1969 when Case introduced the radically redesigned Agri King tractors. Ertl wasted no time in building a replica of this distinctive new tractor. The Case 1070 Agri King was the first in a long series of these sturdy, angular toy Case tractors and formed the basis of one of the toy-collecting hobby's most desirable tractors.

Case introduced a marketing plan for 1970 that put specially painted tractors into the hands of dealers who would demonstrate them to area farmers. The tractors, known as Black Knight Demonstrators, were intended to draw attention to Case's tractors. A rumor was circulated that the Black Knight Demonstrator tractors were hand-built at the factory and tuned for more horsepower than standard Case tractors. Power-conscious farmers put a premium on buying one of the Black Knights when the dealer was through with it.

As part of the program, Ertl built a limited number of specially painted Case 1070 Black Knight Demonstrator tractor toys. The toy became as sought after as the real tractor and is one of the most highly prized Ertl collectible toys.

(above) In 1974, Case changed the colors of its 70 series from Desert Sunset/Flambeau Red to Power White/Power Red. Ertl produced 1370s in both color schemes.

(left) The Agri King was the first 1/64-scale Case tractor.

Ertl built a Case Spirit of '76 to commemorate the introduction of Case's new 1570 and the United States' bicentennial.

The 1/16-scale Fordson tractor was added to the line in 1969. It was produced until the late 1970s.

Case's 70 series tractors were produced in Desert Sunset and Flambeau Red until 1974. Case sold a line of English-built tractors that were white over brown and needed a common color scheme to strengthen brand identity. Case married the two in 1974 and adopted a new Power White/Power Red color scheme for its full line. Ertl produced 1370s in both color schemes.

Case introduced a new model, the 1570, in 1976. To commemorate introduction of its new tractor and the U.S. bicentennial, the 1570 could be ordered from the factory with a special stars and stripes paint scheme. The wildly painted tractor was dubbed the "Spirit of '76." Ertl followed with a 1/16-scale toy 1570 Spirit of '76. Two versions of the toy were made, and one had a stripe of a lighter blue.

Ford toys had always been an anomaly in the Ertl line. Ford's toy tractors were built by Hubley until Ertl took over in 1965 and built them in 1/12 scale. Ford tractors had a reputation for being small, and Ford countered that and insisted that its models should be made large. Ertl only made a few Ford toys, but many other manufacturers

built toys based on various Ford models. Ford toys were still being made in 1/12 scale by Ertl in the late 1970s, but 1/64-scale versions also appeared.

When the television show *Green Acres* became a hit in the late 1960s, Ertl tied its product to the successful show with a 1/16-scale Fordson tractor that was "an actual scale model of the one driven by Eddie Albert and Eva Gabor." Other *Green Acres* toys were a 1/32-scale mini set that included a plow, disc, wagon, spreader, and a Farmall 656 painted green with a white *Green Acres* decal on the hood.

(above) The 9700 was the first Ford 1/64-scale toy. It was originally designed with a PTO unit that prevented the drawbar from being used.

(left) The toy on the left is an early-production 1/64-scale 9700. Notice how the PTO unit prevents access to the drawbar. This is a rather serious defect in a toy tractor.

(below) This Ford 4600 from 1977 is 1/12 scale, but its overall size is small enough that standard 1/16-scale rear wheels are the appropriate size.

(above) The original International 544 came with a wide front axle and a 544 decal.

(right) A version of the International 544 with a narrow front end and no 544 decal was first offered in 1969.

Ertl's first 1/64 toys were in the John Deere historical set that was released in 1967. In the 1970s Ertl made 1/64 toys of other OEM makes, which became very popular. Ertl seemed less concerned about authenticity as it experimented with 1/64 toys. Early mistakes, like applying improper decals for the Allis-Chalmers 7045 and putting a PTO unit on its Ford 9700 that prevented easy access to the drawbar, made the toys less authentic but gave collectors something to search for. Ertl corrected the problems quickly, and these rare toys are sought after by collectors today.

The Farmall 544 was introduced by International in 1968. It was the largest tractor ever produced with a hydrostatic transmission, which was a good reason for it to become an Ertl toy in 1969. It was first presented as a wide-front row crop tractor with a 544 decal on the hood. This early 544 was the only one of the many versions of this model to carry an identifying decal. The 544 chassis was also painted yellow and modeled as the industrial 2644. A narrow-front version with dual rear wheels was offered, as well as narrow-front versions of both tractors equipped with a white-painted mounted loader. The 544 was produced by International through 1973, but the toy remained in the Ertl line for over a decade.

(above) Ertl captured the brute strength of International's Farmall 1256 by adding dual rear wheels, large flotation front tires, and a weight rack with plastic suitcase weights. The cab and straight exhaust stack add to the effect.

(right) The 1256 was nicely detailed and had auto steering and authentic decals. The engine detail is impressive.

The familiar 806 casting appeared in 1968 as a 1256 Turbo with dual wheels, a cab, and automotive steering. It also appeared as an 856 with single wheels and no cab. The big square Farmalls and Internationals were impressive toys.

The most profitable tractor size for American tractor manufacturers was the 90- to 150-horsepower range. These tractors were typically made in the United States and represented the bulk of tractor sales. International Harvester's most popular tractors in the 1970s—the 966, 1066, and 1466—were in that power range. These models were released in 1972 and featured turbocharged engines, hydrostatic transmissions, cabs, and other features that International wanted to promote. They carried either the Farmall or International names. International wanted to phase out the Farmall brand, and all of its toys carried an International decal. While IH made many smaller and a few larger tractors, these remained the three popular sizes for its toys. When these models were upgraded to the 86 series in 1977, Ertl toys followed suit with the 886, 1086, and 1586.

International had three toys based on its 66 series tractors in 1972, which remained through the end of the decade.

Ertl's International 666 was one of its most durable toys and remained in production for 22 years.

In 1972, International replaced the 656 with an upgraded 666, and Ertl soon followed and upgraded its 656. The 1/32 toy was very detailed and had white plastic wheels and wider tires. It remained in production through 1994.

The old 1/32-scale 656 was replaced by the 666 in 1974, and the 544 remained in the catalog through the decade. A 1/64-scale model of the popular 1466 was released in 1976, and a 1/64-scale 1086 followed in 1978.

Ertl offered an additional John Deere tractor, a replica of the big 5020, in 1969. Although John Deere had introduced this brute of a tractor in 1966, it took three years until a toy version was created. The real 5020 was too big for most American farms, but it was a big sturdy toy that could stand up to hard use and was very popular on carpet and sandbox farms. Perhaps to make up for lost time, the Ertl 5020 was in production until 1992. The toy varied in minor details over its life span, and the only major variant was a yellow-painted industrial version.

Ertl's first new toy of the 1970s was a John Deere model D that was modeled after a Vindex cast-iron toy from the 1930s. The Vindex toy had a separate cast-iron driver. Although the Ertl toy didn't have a driver, it had the hole in the seat that secured the driver, just like the Vindex toy. Unlike most Ertl toys, which were diecast in aluminum, the John Deere D was diecast in zinc. Production of the 1/16-scale model D continued into 1989. The model was released in 1/32 scale in 1992.

The model 140 first appeared in 1967 and was still part of the line in 1975. It was packaged with a blade and cart, and also in a grounds-maintenance set that included a scraper, cart, blade, brush, and loader. In an attempt to attract non-farm buyers, John Deere made the tractors available with a white body and Spruce Blue, Sunset Orange, Patio Red, or April Yellow hoods, in addition to the familiar John Deere green in 1969. Deere aggressively sold its rainbow-colored lawn and garden machines and that meant Ertl had to recreate them as toys. In spite of its marketing efforts, buyers preferred their lawn and garden tractors to look like real farm tractors and favored the standard green model. The colored lawn tractor experiment ended in 1971.

(top left) Ertl's first 1/64-scale International toy was this 1466, which was released in 1975.

(top right) The John Deere 5020 was too big for most American farms, but it was a big sturdy toy that could stand up to hard use. It was very popular in the carpet and sandbox farm market and remained in production for 24 years.

(above left) Erlt's John Deere D was a copy of a toy made by the Vindex Company in the 1930s.

(above right) The 140 lawn and garden tractor was still being built in 1975. This is from a set that included a cart and blade. Earlier versions had a metal steering wheel.

The Patio Series toys were available in four colors: Spruce Blue, Sunset Orange, Patio Red, and April Yellow.

Ertl's big toy based on the 7520 was built from 1972 to 1975. It is shown here pulling a John Deere Powerflex disk that was first produced as a toy in 1973.

At the other end of the scale, big articulated tractors were the height of farm power in the early 1970s, and any kid who aspired to be a farmer dreamed of having something as big as John Deere's 175-horsepower 7520. Ertl created a toy 7520 in 1972 that remained in the line until John Deere released its Generation II 8630 in 1975.

John Deere introduced its Generation II tractors in August 1972. There were significant changes under the hood, but the most important change for Ertl was the change in the tractor's look. The hood and fenders were completely restyled and the new Sound Guard body was a popular feature. John Deere heavily promoted the safety and comfort of its optional Sound Guard cab and phased out the narrow-front row crop chassis. Consequently, the toys it requested from Ertl were wide-front models with the cab installed.

Ignoring the examples from International and Allis-Chalmers, John Deere still did not have Ertl put a model designation on its tractors. When Ertl released its toy version of John Deere's new tractor, it could have been any one of several models, depending on the power needs of the sandbox farmer. The 125-horsepower 4430 was by far the most popular John Deere tractor and the one the new toy most closely resembled, so John Deere's flagship toy of the era is called a 4430.

In 1974 the big four-wheel drive articulated 7020 and 7520 tractors were replaced by even-more powerful and newly styled models, the 8430 and 8630. Ertl released a replica of a massive tractor in 1975. Again, the tractor has no model designation, and a floor farmer could pretend it was an 8430 or an 8630.

(above) John Deere's flagship Ertl toy was the 4430, which was released in 1972.

(left) The real 226 horsepower tractor weighed 11 tons. The toy tips the scales at nearly six pounds and is over a foot long.

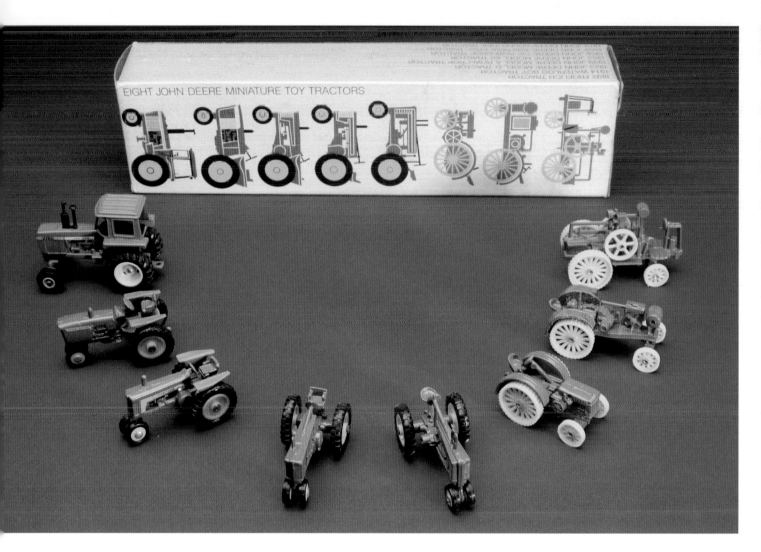

EIGHT JOHN DEERE MINIATURE TOY TRACTORS

This is the eighth 1/64-scale John Deere Historical set, which was released in 1972. It included a Froelich tractor, Waterloo Boy, D, A, 60, 730, 4010, and 4430.

Other manufacturers, notably Allis-Chalmers and International, worked with Ertl to produce replicas of their models in large numbers. John Deere had 11 sizes of tractors in its line in 1975, but they were represented by only four replicas: a 4430, 8630, 2030, and a 140 lawn tractor. The 2030 was the first toy John Deere utility tractor since the 430 of the late 1950s. Real utility tractors were wildly successful, which should have created a market for a utility tractor toy. But the 430 toy didn't sell well, and perhaps that is the reason John Deere declined to have a toy made of any of its utility offerings of the 1960s.

The historical set first introduced in 1967 continued to be popular and evolve. With the introduction of the Generation II tractors in 1972, the eighth version was released. It included a Froelich tractor, Waterloo Boy, D, A, 60, 730, 4010, and 4430.

Plastic model kits of many makes of tractors and implements were introduced in the early 1970s.

Introduced in 1972, John Deere's 2030 was the first toy John Deere utility since the 430 from 1958.

Remote-control toys were the rage in the late 1970s, but they were powered by batteries and were expensive to keep running.

(top) *The Big Ace Allis-Chalmers, Flying Farmall, Farmall 560, and Mighty Minnie Minneapolis-Moline were wildly modified pulling tractors that Ertl offered in 1972.*

(above left) *The Massey-Ferguson 1080 was a six-cylinder tractor, but Ertl assembled some with the V-8 engine of the Model 1150.*

(above right) *This toy Massey-Ferguson 1080 has the correct six-cylinder engine.*

(right) *With its cab, dual rear wheels, and wide front tires, the Massey-Ferguson 1150 is a hefty toy. Some toys were mistakenly assembled with a six-cylinder engine and single rear wheels.*

The John Deere historical set was not Ertl's only departure from diecast replicas. Plastic kits were tried in the early 1970s, and they had mixed results. A wide variety of agricultural tractors and implements were modeled in 1/25-scale polystyrene. They weren't toys, which limited their appeal, and they were of little interest to the emerging farm-toy collecting hobby. Battery-powered radio-controlled toys were tried with some success. They were not popular with parents because they went through a lot of batteries quickly. The modified tractor-pulling hobby was spreading in the United States. in the mid-1970s, and Ertl tapped into this interest by building a set of toy tractor pullers by modifying obsolete models of Minneapolis-Moline, Allis-Chalmers, and Farmall tractors. A decal set was included so that the backyard tractor puller could create his or her unique hot-rod tractor.

Massey-Ferguson wasn't as enthusiastic about toy tractors' marketing potential as other OEMs. Its first toy came out in 1965 and the company didn't solicit a second Ertl agricultural toy until 1970 when the 1080 and 1150 were released. Unfortunately, Massey-Ferguson was the victim of some embarrassing quality-control failures on Ertl's part.

Except for the engines and hood decals, these tractors were similar to the Model 175, and tooling costs were kept low by using the Massey-Ferguson Model 175 body casting. Ertl added a cab and different decals for the 1080. The 1150 was created by adding a cab, grafting plates that resembled a V-8 engine over the six-cylinder engine, and adding dual rear wheels. These variations were haphazardly assembled and resulted in some odd toys of tractors that never existed. Some 1080s were built with V-8 engines, and some had the V-8 plate on one side only. Some 1150s had single rear wheels and a six-cylinder engine. These models are naturally popular among collectors because of the errors. An early V-8-powered tractor, plus the short production run, makes even a properly assembled Massey-Ferguson 1150 toy a valuable Ertl collectible.

(right) This 1/64-scale Massey-Ferguson 2775 was released in 1978.

(below left) The Massey-Ferguson 1155, released in 1973, was the first totally new casting since 1965. Ertl also built a 1/25-scale plastic version of this model and it was chosen as the first Massey-Ferguson 1/64 toy.

(below right) In its search for the right-sized toy, Ertl experimented with 1/20 scale for Massey-Ferguson combines and a few models of tractors.

Massey-Ferguson made a radical change in the looks of its tractors in 1972 with the introduction of the Model 1155. Its square hood and massive grille required an entirely new body casting. Ertl produced toy versions of both the big V-8-powered 1155 and the smaller six-cylinder 1105 in 1973.

Diecast Massey-Ferguson toys were made in 1/16, 1/20, and 1/64 scale. In the early 1970s a Model 760 combine toy was produced. Tractors in 1/64 scale were introduced in the mid-1970s. The early toys were rather crude, but quality rapidly improved.

In 1968 Ertl released a 1/16-scale toy of the new Minneapolis-Moline G-1000. Two versions were built. The first had yellow wheels and a "G-1000" designation on the side. After the real G-1000 went out of production in 1969, Ertl continued to produce a version of the toy with white wheels and no model designation. This toy was sold as the Minneapolis-Moline Deluxe tractor. The 1/16-scale toys were painted in Minneapolis-Moline's bright Energy Yellow. The model of the big tractor was a solid, substantial toy that lasted for years.

When Minneapolis-Moline, which was purchased by White in the early 1960s, was stripped of its autonomy as a separate division in 1969, White began painting Oliver tractors in Minneapolis-Moline colors and vice versa. This blurred the distinction between the two brands. For example, the real Minneapolis-Moline G-1355 was painted green and marketed by White as the Oliver 2155. When Ertl modeled the G-1355, it did its own version of name switching and painted an Oliver 1855 yellow and added Minneapolis-Moline decals and grille, which created an authentic-looking toy that doesn't resemble either real tractor. This toy has the Minneapolis-Moline name on the side, and the grille carries the White name to reflect the ownership of Minneapolis-Moline by White Motors.

New Holland was a short-line manufacturer that built mostly grass-land harvest equipment, but no tractors. Ertl created toy versions of New Holland's baler, combine, swather, spreader, and forage wagon in 1968. Few real farms use exclusively one make of machinery, and having a New Holland implement added to the realism in a rug farmer's machine shed. These toys were not as popular as the full-line machines, and because of their scarcity, they command generally higher prices among collectors.

(top) New Holland's model 907 self-propelled swather was first offered in 1968 and remained in the line through 1972.

(above) New Holland made its name by selling hay balers. Ertl's toy baler was offered for a short time beginning in 1968.

(right) Ertl produced two versions of the Minneapolis-Moline G-1000. The first was a fairly faithful reproduction with "G-1000" on the side. After the real G-1000 went out of production in 1969, the toy appeared with white wheels and no model designation.

The Minneapolis-Moline G 1355 resembles an Oliver 1855 more than any Minneapolis-Moline model.

The Oliver 1850 was replaced by the White-Oliver 1855 in 1970.

The Oliver 1850 was upgraded to the 1855 in 1970. The tractor was only slightly different, but there were big differences behind the scenes. A reformation of the White Corporation in 1969 resulted in a change of brand name to White Oliver. Beginning in 1970, Oliver green tractors sporadically carried the White name in addition to the Oliver name until the Oliver brand was dropped entirely in 1976.

In the 1970s the real tractors were getting larger, and so were the scale toys. A 1954 1/16-scale John Deere 60 weighed 1 1/4 pounds. The 1970s Massey-Ferguson 1150 of the same scale weighed just over five pounds. The toys were getting more expensive and they were harder for small children to play with. They were also more likely to cause injury when thrown or dropped on

a child. Ertl tried some 1/20-scale Massey-Ferguson tractors to keep the size of the toys down, but the scale was not popular enough to become a new standard. A few 1/32-scale toys, which were popular in Europe, were tried, but they didn't catch on in the United States. Ertl experimented with a few 1/64-scale toys in the 1970s, and it was with that scale that Ertl found a new market.

Another new market was developing, but Ertl was unaware of it at the time. Adults who had grown up with Ertl toys started to buy old toys like the ones they played with as children. The hobby of toy collecting was gathering momentum, and in 1978, it found a center in Lamour, South Dakota.

This Oliver 1855 with duals and ROPS does not carry the White name.

Chapter Five

The Collector Era

The beginning of a phenomenon that remade the farm-toy industry happened in 1978. In the 1970s a worldwide movement quietly grew among farm-toy enthusiasts. Driven by nostalgia, adult collectors hunted down and bought toys like the ones they had played with as children. Thus, a nationwide network of toy collectors developed. In 1978, Claire and Cathy Scheibe of LaMoure, South Dakota, started a newsletter to link the hobbyists and organized an annual farm-toy show in Ertl's hometown of Dyersville, Iowa, to bring them all together. To commemorate the first event, the Scheibes had Ertl build 500 special toys for show attendees. The toy was a Farmall 560 modified with a wagon-steered wide-front axle and an inscription of "11-1-78" cast into the frame. Previously, special toys had been made as promotional items for OEM dealers, but this Farmall 560 was the first toy made specifically for farm-toy enthusiasts. These enthusiasts opened a market that eventually outstripped both OEM dealer and toy store markets.

The interest in collecting Ertl toys mushroomed in the early 1980s. New toy collectors joined the hobby every day. The *Toy Farmer* newsletter quickly grew to a magazine with thousands of subscribers and helped spread the hobby all over North America.

The value of early toys went through the roof and collectors clamored for something affordable to collect. Toy shows popped up all over the country where collectors bought and sold old toys. Ertl fed the hobby by building special commemorative toys for these events, and the toys became the first new collector's items. The biggest event was the annual National Farm Toy Show in Dyersville, Iowa, which drew thousands of participants.

Toys for OEM manufacturers were still a major part of Ertl's business, but fortunately for Ertl, the business was driven by collectors more and more every year. The farm-equipment industry was about to face the largest reshuffling in 20 years, which resulted in the disappearance of familiar names. The added sales to collectors kept business booming at Ertl in spite of the elimination of old OEM accounts.

(opposite top) The 1978 National Farm Toy Show Farmall 560 was the first toy made specifically for toy tractor collectors.

(opposite bottom) The second National Farm Toy Show tractor began what became standard procedure for Collector Edition releases. A new toy was released in 1979 with an inscription cast into the frame and a medallion on the hood. It was released as a shelf model in 1980.

A conflict existed between the interests of the manufacturers and the interests of toy collectors. OEMs wanted toys in their dealerships to increase traffic and build brand loyalty, plus with collector interest growing, there was a good profit to be made selling toys. They did not want their toys sold at toy shows. Collectors wanted to buy new toys at shows and some wanted to support their hobby by selling new toys at the shows. Ertl just wanted to sell more toys, and the more outlets there were, the better the chances of that happening.

A system was agreed upon where Ertl would build special Collector Editions of selected new tractors that would only be available from OEM dealers. These dealers would have exclusive rights to all new shelf-model issues for a specific period of time, which was typically one year. After the period of exclusivity was up, licensed toy dealers could market the shelf models at shows.

When a new tractor model was announced, the OEM would inform its dealers that a collector model of that tractor would be available. Some OEMs allowed their dealers to order a fixed number of collector tractors. For others, a collector toy was available for order for a certain period of time, typically a couple of months. When the order period was over, Ertl built the number of collector toys that had been requested.

The OEMs weren't introducing new tractors fast enough to supply the demands of collectors, so Ertl added a new dimension to its farm-toy business. It introduced the first of a line of 1/16-scale replicas of vintage tractors in 1984. In cooperation with John Deere, Ertl released a toy version of the John Deere model A tractor that was built from 1934 through 1937. Ertl built two versions—a shelf model that was economical, could be played with, and was built in large quantities; and a Collector Edition that was built in smaller quantities and not intended for children. This was the beginning of a practice that Ertl followed for years. Vintage toys were released first as a Collector Edition that was available only at OEM dealerships, and then they were released as a shelf model that could be sold by any authorized Ertl retailer.

The Collector Editions typically were produced with different features than the shelf model. A shelf model might cost $18 or $19, while the Collector Edition usually cost

$30. For example, the John Deere A Collector Edition had steel wheels, but the shelf model came with rubber tires. This gave collectors something different to buy, although they weren't necessarily better. In terms of authenticity, some enthusiasts actually thought they were worse. Detail and workmanship were no better, and many had nonauthentic chrome decals.

(above) Ertl began production of 1/16-scale vintage tractors in 1984 with the John Deere model A. This is the shelf model of that toy.

(left) The Case VAC toys released in 1988 were typical of Ertl's new vintage toys. The Collector's Edition had a black smokestack and steering wheel, a single front wheel, a diecast inscription in the frame, and chrome decals. The shelf model retailed for less than $20, while the Collector's Edition retailed for about $30.

(above) This 1/64-scale Deutz-Allis 8070 is identical to the Allis-Chalmers 8070 except for the decal on the hood.

(right) The Deutz-Allis 6240 toy depicts the first tractor from the new company to be painted Spring Green.

Ertl built Allis-Chalmers 7000 and 8000 tractors in the early 1980s, but Allis-Chalmers was in serious financial trouble. By 1985, the tractor and Gleaner combine divisions had been sold to Klockner-Humbolt-Deutz, and the name of the West Allis, Wisconsin, company was changed to Deutz-Allis. Deutz-Allis put its name on the old Allis-Chalmers models, but they were otherwise unchanged. Ertl switched its Allis-Chalmers 8010s and 8030s to the Deutz-Allis name almost immediately.

Deutz-Allis soon ended Allis-Chalmers tractor production and imported Deutz tractors from Germany. Ertl quickly tooled up to make toys based on the German tractors. The first Spring Green Deutz-Allis toy tractors, the 6260 with front-wheel assist and the 6240, appeared in 1985. Other models soon followed. The orange Deutz-Allis toys were dropped from the line in 1988. In 1989 and 1990, Deutz-Allis designed the 9100 series of 150-plus horsepower tractors, which were assembled in Ohio. Ertl created a replica of the big green 9150 in 1989.

The Deutz 9150 was built in Ohio using a German air-cooled engine and an American-designed and-built drivetrain.

(above) The first Allis-
Chalmers vintage replica
was the WD-45, which
came in a wide-front
Collector's Edition, as
well as the narrow-front
shelf model.

(right) At the request of
Deutz-Allis, this handsome
Allis-Chalmers D-21 was
released as a Collector's
Edition in 1987. The D-21
appeared in several
configurations over the
next 15 years.

Americans remembered Allis-Chalmers fondly, and there was still a good market for Allis-Chalmers toys, but none were being produced. In 1985 Deutz-Allis allowed Ertl to produce vintage Allis-Chalmers replicas to fill the demand. The first 1/16-scale vintage Allis-Chalmers replica was the WD-45, which was released in 1985. Other revered Allis-Chalmers models followed on a roughly annual basis.

Ertl created its first 1/64-scale self-propelled combine, a Gleaner R50, in 1987. Previous small Ertl combines had been 1/80 scale, but the popularity of 1/64 encouraged the company to produce its combines in this slightly larger size. Existing 1/80 combines continued to be produced, but new issues were 1/64.

(above) Ertl's Caterpillar Challenger 65 (rear) was the first toy Challenger and Ertl's first 1/64-scale collector's tractor. The 85C was released in 1993, and the 45, with Caterpillar's new styling, came out in 1994.

(left) The Gleaner R50 was Ertl's first 1/64-scale self-propelled combine. It was released in 1987.

(above) Case's 2590 was created as a shelf model (rear) and a collector's edition in 1979. The collector's edition included a serial number, decal, silver muffler, and other details.

(right) What's a tractor without a plow? Ertl created appropriate implements to accompany its tractors to the sandbox.

Ertl had built Caterpillar construction toys since the early 1960s, but Caterpillar machinery had seen only limited use in agriculture. In 1986 the company thrust itself into the center of farm-tractor business with the revolutionary rubber-tracked Challenger 65. The Challenger started a rubber-tracked tractor revolution. Its replica of the Challenger 65 was the first 1/64 Collector Edition toy offered by Ertl. The Collector's Edition included a diecast inscription and specially labeled blister card. Production of the Collector's Edition was limited to 5,000 units. The market for Caterpillar toys was limited due to the relatively small number of agricultural tractors the company sold. Ertl's subsequent release of new Caterpillar toys was similarly limited.

In 1978 Case replaced the 70 series tractors with the 90 series, which had a whole new look. Ertl re-created the 2390 and 2590 in 1/16 scale. The tractors were big, and Ertl also made several 1/32-scale toys of tractors in the series. Toy collectors were beginning to be noticed by OEMs and Ertl in the late 1970s. Case allowed a special Collector Edition of the shelf model 2590 to be created and released in April 1979. The Collector Edition included a serial number, special decal, and detail changes. Only 1,500 of these toys were made.

The Ford TW-60 and
Steiger Couger were the
same toy with different
paint and decals.

Ford was still a power in the U.S. tractor industry in the 1980s, but the hard times weakened the company. Low sales reduced the appeal of Ford toys, and although Ford maintained a full line of tractors, only a few models were released as toys. Many of its smaller models were imported, and production of its mid-size models was moved to England in 1985.

With no facilities to build big articulated tractors, Ford filled its product line by buying them from the Steiger Company in Fargo, North Dakota. The real tractors were Steiger models that were painted in Ford colors. Mirroring the real thing, Ertl's 1/16-scale Ford TW-60 was merely a Steiger Cougar toy with different paint and decals.

Fords were popular overseas, and Ertl built some Ford models in 1/32 scale for the European market. Ertl built a 1/16-scale Ford tractor in 1982. European toy makers built a proprietary type of hitches to attach implements to their tractors, and Ertl attempted to make its toys compatible with the European implements. The result was a clumsy mechanism on the back of the toy that completely ruined the notion of realism.

(top left) The Ford 5000 was released in 1988 in both a collector's and a shelf version. The real tractor was produced with both blue and gray hoods. Ertl used that to distinguish between the Collector's Edition (gray) and the shelf model (blue).

(top right) This Ford TW35 was released in 1984 and is a relatively scarce toy today. Ford tractors experienced declining popularity in the United States at the time, and sales of Ford toys were limited.

(middle left) In the late 1980s and early 1990s, Ertl 1/32-scale toys, like this Ford TW-5, were built to be compatible with Britains LTD toys. It had a bulky and complex three-point hitch that didn't look authentic or work well.

(middle right) This 7710 Stage II is a replica of the tractor built after production was moved to England.

(bottom left) U.S.-built Ford tractors, like this 1710, had a light blue stripe on the hood. When production was moved to England, the stripe was changed to black.

(bottom right) Fittingly, the first vintage Ford tractor from Ertl was a replica of the 8N, the most popular Ford tractor of all time.

Ertl's next Ford vintage tractor was the 1988 release of the Model 5000. The real tractor was produced with both blue and gray hoods. Ertl used this fact to distinguish between the Collector Edition, which had a gray hood, and the shelf model, which had a blue hood.

Toys in 1/64-scale rapidly gained favor among floor farmers and collectors alike. By the mid-1980s, sales of 1/64 toys surpassed sales of 1/16-scale toys. The size and detail suffered, but the lower price meant you could afford to buy more models. Ertl expanded its 1/64 tractor and implement lines in 1985 when it bought Mini Toys Inc., a toy manufacturer in Guttenberg, Iowa. The purchase brought licensed brand names into the Ertl fold, including Hesston and Mitsubishi tractors and several toy implements. The Hesston line included the Hesston 100 and 130 tractors.

International introduced a radical new idea in farm tractors in 1978 when it released the 3388 2+2 row crop. In 1979 it produced the 3588, a more powerful version of this unique articulated tractor, and Ertl replicated it in a toy. The first 3,200 of these models had the words "First Series" cast into the frame, and the toy came with a special stand. One was offered to each IH dealer.

The 2+2 design was promoted heavily, but it was still resisted by farmers. Ertl released a 1/64-scale version of the 3588 in 1981, and a 1/16-scale toy of the 6388 in 1983.

International Harvester began to design replacements for its big tractors in 1976. At a meeting in Kansas City in September 1981, IH introduced a new line of tractors with bold, square styling and all-new mechanical systems. Known as the 50 series, IH called its tractors the "New Number One" and had every intention to become America's number one tractor manufacturer. Ertl was there with a commemorative

Ertl acquired the license to build this Hesston field-chopper outfit in 1985 when it bought Mini Toys.

(above) The first 3,200 toys of the 3588 2+2 tractors had "first series" cast into the frame. One copy with a display stand was available to each IH dealer.

(left) The 3588 came out in 1/64 scale in 1981. It was a sturdy toy; plastic was used only on its wheels. This well-used example has a few scrapes, but it is ready to plow the sandbox.

(above) The Cub was popular and relatively inexpensive. International produced the Cub Cadet in both International red and Cadet yellow.

(right) The International 5288, released in 1981, was the second of the three 50 series tractors produced by Ertl.

1/16-scale 5088 toy. The toy had dual rear wheels and "First Edition KC 9-81" engraved in the frame. Ertl eventually rendered all three 50 series tractors, the 5088, 5288, and 5488, as toys.

The first 1/16-scale vintage International from Ertl was the Farmall 300 that was released in 1984. The next year the toy was given a wagon-steered wide-front axle, a white-painted grille, and some new decals to become a 350.

The new tractors weren't enough to save International. The company continued to have financial problems, and Case bought out the struggling farm equipment line in 1985. Case's problem was what to do with two iconic names in tractors and two complete model lines. It solved the problem by adopting some machines from each line, changing its name to Case IH, and adopting the red and black IH colors.

Ertl created the Farmall 350 by modifying a 300. Like most Ertl vintage tractors, it was available in a Collector's Edition, which featured a narrow front end, white wheels, and black stacks.

(above) Case adopted International's colors for its tractors after it bought International. The tractor on the left is a 1984 Case 2594, and a 1985 Case-IH 2594 is on the right.

(right) Case introduced its new red color with this 1/16-scale Case IH 2594, which was presented in a special gift box to each attendee at the 1985 dealer meeting held in Las Vegas.

(top left) The smaller Case IH 94 series of tractors were handsome machines, and Ertl rendered them in excellent detail.

(top right) The interior of the Case IH 2394 included a seat, control levers, and a complete dashboard.

(above left) This 1/64-scale Case IH combine was packed with both a grain and a corn head in 1988. The same toy with a commemorative sticker was sold at the 1989 Husker Harvest Show.

(above right) This 1/64 Case IH 2594 was sold as a souvenir of the Farm Progress Show in Knightstown, Indiana. The name "Farm Progress" does not appear on the toy or packaging.

The shelf model 4450 did not carry a model designation. This Special Edition model was built to commemorate the 75th anniversary of the Syracuse Branch. The 6,200 toys that were made were available only to dealers in that area.

Case IH was enthusiastic about promotion through farm toys. It collaborated with Ertl to make toys of many of its tractors and implements. By the mid-1980s, there were many 1/64-scale toy tractors and implements available, including various versions of combines, cotton pickers, balers, and farm machines that could never have been economically built in 1/16 scale. Although International went out of business in 1985, Ertl has continued to bring back popular IH tractors from the past.

Case IH bought the Steiger Company in Fargo, North Dakota, in 1987 and built big articulated tractors there. Ertl built models of its Case IH 9150 in 1/32 scale.

For over 20 years John Deere had been the best-selling brand in the country, so it is no surprise that John Deere was one of the most collectible brands of toy tractor. Demand was high, but John Deere continued its policy of allowing only a few current models to be replicated. When the vintage toy program was instituted, John Deere participated with enthusiasm. Beginning in 1984, at least one vintage John Deere Collector Edition tractor was released each year.

New John Deere tractors were still being produced for the sandbox. The company introduced the most extensive new line of tractors in its history in 1982. Eleven new models of tractors were introduced, and many were built overseas. As usual, John Deere chose one of the medium-size row crop tractors from its Waterloo, Iowa, plant to be the centerpiece of its toy program. The 140-horsepower 4450 was expected to be the company's biggest seller, so it was chosen as the tractor to be modeled by Ertl.

(above) John Deere's first 1/64-scale combine was this Model 9500 Maxi. It is shown here with a generic wagon and a Model 4450 tractor from 1986.

(right) John Deere's 1/32-scale Model 3140 was a popular model in both the United States and Europe.

(far right) Ertl reached far back into the beginning of John Deere's history when it created the replica Waterloo Boy in 1987.

Ertl moved into the European market and its effort was assisted by John Deere's tractor-sourcing program. Many of John Deere's utility tractors were built and sold in Europe, so the toys that represented these models would have European features. Through its long production life, versions of the model 3140 exhibited an interesting mix of European and American characteristics. It was built in 1/32 scale, the most popular European scale, and it came with a European-style square cab. In 1982 it was available with an American-style sound guard cab. It was equipped with a European-style three-point hitch in the late 1980s to make it compatible with Britain's toys. A feature of European toys that was never characteristic of U.S. toys was that the cab was often removable. In the early 1990s, Ertl built a 3140 with an American-style removable cab. Although the real tractor was only produced from 1980 to 1984, Ertl built the toy through 1993.

(top left) Ertl released a shelf model and a Collector's Edition of an unstyled John Deere G in July 1987. The Collector's Edition had steel wheels, taller stacks, chrome mylar decals, and a collector's inscription. The taller stacks were an acknowledgment that the tractor would probably not be played with, and that authenticity was more important than child safety.

(top right) John Deere tried several scales for its toy combines before this 1/20-scale Titan II came out in 1985.

(middle left) John Deere continued to promote its lawn and garden line with this Model 200 lawn tractor from 1988.

(middle right) Ertl celebrated its 40th anniversary by making a commemorative model similar to the first John Deere toy it created in 1945.

(bottom) Collectors look for anything unique in a toy. A number of 1/64-scale John Deere 8050s were painted the wrong shade of green (left), which makes them a desirable item among collectors.

Ertl built a selection of 1/43-scale replicas that were nicely detailed, but they didn't catch on with collectors.

Always searching for new markets, Ertl released the first of a series of 1/43-scale vintage replicas in 1984. This first replica was a Farmall 300 created for the 1984 National Farm Toy Show. Many makes and models were subsequently rendered in the small scale. The replicas were nicely detailed and carefully packaged. Although a wide variety of tractors were represented in the series, it was never popular among collectors. The last Ertl 1/43-scale tractor was a John Deere 4230 produced for *Toy Farmer* magazine in 1998.

Massey-Ferguson's representation in Ertl toys continued to be sparse. Many of the company's toys were in the unpopular 1/20 scale, but there were some 1/64 toys of interest. A 4880 was released in 1981, followed by several versions of the 699 in 1984, and finally the newly restyled 3070 was released in 1989.

Hasbro wanted to purchase Ertl from Kidde in March 1987, but the sale did not take place. The British-American company Hanson PLC purchased Kidde, including Ertl, in late 1987. As the company changed hands again, its toy business kept growing.

In the course of a decade, Ertl's business environment shifted dramatically. Through the 1970s, the market had been OEM manufacturers. Ertl built what the manufacturers wanted to sell in their dealerships. This began to change in the late 1970s, and by the late 1980s, it was driven by collectors. But the landscape was still changing. The interest in replicas of vintage tractors created opportunities for other toy manufacturers, particularly Scale Models and SpecCast, to make inroads in a market that Ertl had enjoyed exclusively for decades.

In 1986 a business group from Dyersville, Iowa, with the support of Claire Scheibe of *Toy Farmer* magazine, and Fred Ertl Jr., broke ground for the National Farm Toy Museum. The goal of the museum is to tell the story of farming through displays of farm toys. The National Farm Toy Museum displays over 30,000 farm toys. To raise funds for the project, Ertl produced a set of four 1/16-scale Cockshutt tractors. The set was snapped up and collectors clamored for more. A second set of Cockshutts was produced for the museum the next year. Tractor sets and Special Edition tractors continue to be created for the benefit of the museum.

(above) Ertl released the model 3070 toys, with both single and dual rear wheels, in 1989.

(above left) The most popular Massey-Ferguson toys from the 1980s were 1/64 scale, like this Model 4880.

(above) The first National Farm Toy Museum set consisted of a Cockshutt 40, Cockshutt 50, and a Blackhawk 40.

(opposite) Ertl chose newer-model Cockshutt tractors for the second National Farm Toy Museum set—a 560, 570, and 570 Super.

As more models with greater detail came onto the market, collectors began to complain that Ertl's offerings lacked detail and authenticity. Collectors convinced the company to drop the chrome decals on their Collector Editions in 1988. Computerized machining of casting dies made it cheaper to include finer detail, which Ertl quickly incorporated in its replicas, but that wasn't enough.

Ertl began to face competition from custom builders. These men and women hand-built farm-toy replicas with extraordinary detail and craftsmanship. The toys sold for a lot of money. A single custom-built tractor could sell for hundreds of dollars. Ertl had plans in the works to meet this challenge by creating a toy like nothing the company had ever produced.

Chapter Six

A New Precision in Toys

Ertl was still the largest and best-known toy-replica manufacturer in the world in 1990, but its crown was beginning to tarnish. In mid-1990 Ertl introduced a replica that changed all of that.

Ertl chose an important old tractor to introduce its important new idea. The old tractor was the John Deere model A. The new idea was Precision Classic replicas. While Collector Edition replicas were toys that had been given a little extra attention, the Precision Series replicas were not toys in any form. They were highly detailed, 1/16-scale models constructed of hundreds of separate parts and carefully finished. They were shipped in a package that included a collector medallion and a reproduction of a historical brochure.

The Precision Classic John Deere model A cost about $75 in 1990. Buyers who were used to paying $20 or $30 for a shelf model were in shock. A Precision Farmall Regular was released for a similar price that same year. Thinking the price was an aberration, collectors did not immediately take to the high-priced Precision replicas. The next year Ertl released the Precision Classic John Deere model A with a set of extremely detailed cultivators, and the price was even higher at $115. Collectors finally understood, and although the price seemed high, the Precision replicas were a good value and the price was not unreasonable.

(opposite) Ertl's Precision John Deere A introduced an unprecedented level of detail.

(above) The Precision Classic John Deere A with rubber tires and cultivators was the most expensive tractor replica Ertl had produced at that time. Only John Deeres in this series are referred to as Precision Classics. All others are Precision Series replicas.

Ertl introduced Precision Series implements in 1991 with the two-bottom Little Genius plow.

When the next Precision toy was released, sales improved and the Precision line became a success. Ertl released its first Precision implement, an International Little Genius two-bottom plow, in 1991. In 14 years, over 70 tractors and implements have been rendered in Ertl's Precision Series.

On the OEM front, the Deutz-Allis effort was not going well. Although big OEM companies had imported farm tractors for years, they were styled and painted like the American-built tractors whose names they shared. American farmers were skeptical of the totally foreign lime-green Deutz-Allis tractors. In 1990 members of Deutz-Allis management formed the Allis-Gleaner Corporation (AGCO).

In an attempt to tap into the loyalty of American farmers, the new management painted the tractors a color similar to the familiar Allis-Chalmers Persian Orange with dark blue chassis. Otherwise the tractors were the same and still carried the Deutz-Allis name, which was a gift to Ertl and toy collectors. Ertl was able to create a whole new line of toys by changing paint colors.

In 1989 the Ertl Company announced the Collector Edition 1/16-scale toy Allis-Chalmers Roto-Baler. The shelf model was released in early 1990. This was Ertl's first vintage implement and the toy maker's first implement released as a Collector Edition and a shelf model. The Collector Edition included a gray bale belt, special decals, and a diecast inscription.

AGCO quickly gathered Hesston, White, Massey-Ferguson, and numerous short-line and foreign makes of farm machinery into the fold. Within five years, AGCO had made itself the recipient of the legacy of much of North American tractor history. It held the remnants of Oliver, Minneapolis-Moline, White, Cockshutt, Allis-Chalmers, Rumely, Massey-Harris, and Massey-Ferguson. Of all those venerated brands, only White and Massey-Ferguson were still in production, and that didn't last for long.

Because Deutz-Allis owned the Allis-Chalmers trademark, the Roto-Baler replica was only available at Deutz-Allis dealers.

(above) Allis-Chalmers D-19 was
built for the 1989 National Farm
Toy Show and was released as a
shelf model in 1990.

(right) In mid-1990, the Deutz-
Allis 9150 traded its Deutz green
paint for a more familiar color—
Persian Orange.

White Farm Equipment had been in business since the late 1960s. Ertl declined to build White toys and left that market to Scale Models. AGCO bought the White line of tractors in 1991, and by 1992, Ertl built its first and only White toys. White Farm Equipment attempted to capitalize on the heritage of the tractor companies by offering its Model 60 and 80 tractors in Oliver green, Minneapolis Moline yellow, Cockshutt red, or White silver. Production of most small- and medium-size tractors had been moved overseas. These were the smallest models still built in the United States, and White proudly called them the Spirit of America series. This was a perfect opportunity for Ertl to create a set of tractors to market. Ertl only offered two White products, the 1/64-scale Model 60 and Model 80 Spirit of America sets.

(above) Ertl made two White Spirit of America sets in 1992: a set of Model 80s and this set of Model 60s.

(left) When Oregon farmer Bob Bafus ordered five Big Bud tractors from the factory in blue, his favorite color, it gave Ertl the opportunity to create a new Big Bud toy.

The real Big Bud 440 weighed 20 tons and had 440 horsepower.

The popularity of smaller scales gave Ertl the opportunity to build a wider variety of toys, including toys from small, independent OEMs. In 1993 Ertl built 1/64-scale Big Bud tractors. All Big Bud tractors were huge—the smallest weighed 17 tons—and Ertl declined to build them in 1/16 scale.

Case IH introduced three world tractors in 1990, the Maxxum series. These medium-size tractors were designed to appeal to farmers all over the world. Ertl built replicas of Maxxum tractors in the 1/64 and 1/16 scales to appeal to the U.S. market and the 1/32 scale that was popular in Europe.

Fred Ertl Jr. retired in 1992 after seeing his company grow from a basement operation in his family home to multimillion-dollar international company. It had passed through several owners, but Fred Jr.'s vision kept the company on a steady track. The 50th anniversary of the company's founding was in 1995 and Ertl celebrated by building Special Edition toys and tractor sets that commemorated the occasion. The Milestone set contained a 1940s Ford 9N, a 1950s Allis-Chalmers WD, a 1950s John Deere 620LP, a 1970s International 966, a 1980s Massey-Ferguson 3140, and a Caterpillar Challenger 65 from the 1990s. This was the first time Ertl had ever sold different makes of tractors in the same retail package.

(top left) Case IH celebrated the introduction of the Maxxum series and had Ertl render replicas of all three models. This 1/16-scale 5140 with MFWD is a Special Edition that was released in 1990.

(top right) This 1/64-scale toy from 1990 represents the new Case IH, the 9260.

(below) The Ertl Farmall H replica was as popular as the real thing. First released in 1985 as a Special Edition, it continued as a shelf model, several more Special Editions, and even appeared in a number of play sets.

Case IH's line began to change in 1992 with the redesigned Maxxum series. By 1995 the entire line had been redesigned and Ertl redesigned its replicas to match. Ertl built over a dozen models of the new series of tractors in 1/64, 1/32, and 1/16 scale, but it no longer had exclusive rights to build Case IH toys. For years small, mostly European, companies nibbled at the edges of Ertl's U.S. market. But in 1995, Scale Models built 1/16 and 1/64 replicas of selected Case IH models in direct competition with Ertl. Scale Models had one advantage over Ertl. Most of Ertl's products were being manufactured in China, Korea, or other Asian manufacturing centers, while Scale Models chose to build its replicas in the United States, a corporate decision that appealed to American buyers.

Case IH had a busy vintage program with Ertl from the moment the company was created. One vintage toy joined the line of contemporary toys in 1985, but by 1992, only one new contemporary toy was introduced, while six new vintage toys joined the product line.

One of several special products Ertl produced for its 50th anniversary was this set of six tractors that illustrate the evolution of farm tractors during Ertl's existence.

International Harvester replicas of the 1960s and early 1970s were still popular. Ertl released six new toys based on the 66 series International toys in the early 1990s, which was more than were made when the tractors were new. Those models weren't enough of the big red Internationals to satisfy collectors, so in 1996, in conjunction with the *Toy Tractor Times* magazine and Case IH, Ertl released Special Edition 1456. These square-hooded tractors remained favorites with collectors, and more models in different scales were produced, which culminated in a 1/16 Precision Series 1466.

(top) This shelf model 706 followed a Special Edition onto the market in 1995.

(above) Toys like this 1/64-scale Hesston swather helped toy tractor enthusiasts create realistic farm scenes.

(above) Ertl built this Special Edition International 1456 for the Toy Tractor Times in 1996.

In the late 1980s John Deere began to identify its toys by model numbers, which provided Ertl with opportunities to produce more toys for John Deere dealers to sell. Toys had become a year-round profit center for John Deere dealers, and having more toys on the shelf helped their bottom lines. John Deere's line of toy tractors had grown from two in the 1960s to over 30 in the 1990s, and that's just the tractors. Toys and replicas of implements and other John Deere products swelled the catalogs to over 100 items. For as long as John Deere has built articulated tractors, Ertl has rendered one as a toy. In 1996 John Deere introduced its 260-horsepower 9200. The real thing cost $128,000, but a rug farmer on a budget could get a 1/16-scale Ertl replica that met safety criteria for less than $100.

The 9200 articulated tractor with triple wheels was John Deere's big tractor in the late 1990s. The toy weighed nearly six pounds.

John Deere incorporated a radical new idea, modular construction, in its 6000/7000 series of tractors. The time a broken tractor spent in the repair shop was a major expense for a farmer. As tractors became larger and more complex, this became a larger problem. John Deere's modular construction grouped major component systems together on the tractor so they could be accessed and replaced quickly and easily. It was such a radical idea that John Deere worked with the designers at Ertl to produce a 1/16-scale instructional model of a John Deere 7800 to demonstrate the modular concept. The diecast and plastic model was broken down into the service modules and packed in a special see-through box. Three special versions of the tractor were made for John Deere, and two versions were made for sale to the public through John Deere dealers. A fully assembled shelf model 7800 was released in 1993.

The interest in antique farm tractors of all makes began to increase rapidly in the 1980s. The Two-Cylinder Club for antique John Deere tractor enthusiasts had organized in the mid-1980s and grew into one of the largest clubs. The Two-Cylinder club held periodic expos, and in cooperation with Ertl and John Deere, had a Special Edition vintage John Deere toy created for each one. In order to keep costs low, the tooling was designed so it could be used at a later date to build a similar shelf model and increase the pool of interesting John Deere models built by Ertl.

(above) John Deere's 7800 demonstrated the modular service concept. It was a snap-together toy for adults.

(left) The 7800 was also created in a toy-rated shelf model.

The Two-Cylinder Club had Ertl build a John Deere 620 Orchard tractor for its second expo. Orchard tractors are low and streamlined so they can travel near trees without damaging the branches.

It seemed no one was immune from the farm-machinery industry's series of bankruptcies and buyouts. In 1985 Ford purchased the short-line company Sperry-New Holland and created Ford-New Holland. Two years later, Ford-New Holland purchased Versatile 4wd Company, and Fiat purchased Ford-New Holland from Ford Motors in 1990. The firm's tractors retained the Ford name until the year 2000, but New Holland tractors appeared almost immediately. It was a bad time for Ford toy tractors. Few people were interested in the Ford name.

In 1998 Ertl purchased Britains, the most popular toy manufacturer in Europe. Britains had a large catalog of 1/32-scale toys, and Ertl retained the Britains brand while consolidating some of the products. All scales are sold globally, but Ertl's new 1/32 offerings are primarily branded Britains but carry a smaller Ertl logo. The 1/16 and 1/64 toys popular in the United States carry the Ertl logo but also include the Britains brand. With the purchase of Britains, Ertl became the largest toy manufacturer in the world, and it was about to become bigger.

(top left) The International 1 PR corn picker was the second vintage implement from Ertl and was released in 1990. The John Deere 12A combine was released in 1991 as a collector's edition, and later as a shelf model.

(top right) The New Holland 8160 appeared in 1996. The last new Ford toy from Ertl was the 8670, which was built in 1997.

(middle left) Even shelf models were becoming more detailed. An opening hood that revealed a detailed engine was a more common feature.

(middle right) This gold-painted Special Edition was built for the 1995 New Holland dealer parts expo.

It was released in the spring of 1995. The toy is a replica of the gold painted Ford 901 dealer demonstrator of the 1950s. Each New Holland dealer could order up to 60 units of the toy. The diecast inscription says "New Holland Parts Expo Special Edition."

(bottom left) The first Ford 9N replica from Ertl was all gray and was made in 1988. In 1993, a Special Edition version was built for the Toy Tractor Times that simulated a polished aluminum hood.

(bottom right) A Special Edition of the Ford 641 Workmaster was created for the Toy Tractor Times in 1998. This was the first replica of the 641.

115

Chapter Seven

New Ownership, Again

In 1999 Ertl was sold once again to Racing Champions. Racing Champions is a builder of race-car replicas in 1/64 and 1/24 scale with a history of extensive and aggressive marketing. Ertl and Racing Champions combined to form Racing Champions Ertl Corporation. Racing Champions' principal business is the toy and collectible market, which bodes well for the future of Ertl. Ertl has become the core property of a corporation, rather than being a peripheral part.

AGCO's efforts at consolidation had eliminated the White and Deutz-Allis brands and created AGCO-White and AGCO-Allis for a short time. New names on old tractors would have been a bonanza for Ertl and require only paint and decals to produce a whole new toy, but it did not have exclusive rights. Ertl made only a few 1/64-scale AGCO toys.

By 2001, AGCO had shuffled and reshuffled its brands so that in the U.S. market it was down to Massey-Ferguson and AGCO. In 2002 AGCO acquired the Challenger name from Caterpillar. Ertl built one series of 1/64-scale toys that represented the 225-horsepower offerings from AGCO. Although they had different engines, these tractors looked similar, and Ertl produced three different replicas by applying different paint and decals to the same castings.

(above) Ertl produced this colorful trio of 1/64 AGCO brands in 2003.

(opposite) The AGCO-Allis brand only existed for a few years. Ertl made one toy that carried the name, and it was released as a 6690 shelf model and a 6670 Special Edition.

Scale Models built replicas of current AGCO models, but Ertl still created vintage toys under license from AGCO. With its extensive list of old American farm-tractor trademarks, AGCO was a rich source of material. Ertl had already built seven successful Precision Series Allis-Chalmers and Oliver replicas when it introduced a stunning toy in 2001. Part of AGCOs heritage was New Idea, a short-line manufacturer of harvesting equipment. Ertl paired a New Idea mounted corn picker with an Allis-Chalmers D-17 to produce its most intricate and colorful replica.

In 2003 Ertl reached back to the 1950s and produced two beautiful Precision Series replicas of vintage AGCO-owned trademarks. The prices of Precision Series replicas had steadily increased to over $100 for a basic tractor.

The Toy Tractor Times *anniversary tractors were launched in 1986.*
The magazine offers a unique collectible tractor every year, which are
most often built by Ertl. The 2000 tractor was this Allis-Chalmers 7045.

Another shakeup in the tractor industry happened on May 15, 1999. The Italian company Fiat, which owned Ford-New Holland, purchased Case IH. The new company became Case-New Holland (CNH). CNH brought the heritage of Case, Ford, International Harvester, New Holland, Steiger, and Versatile together. Mergers and buyouts had resulted in only three OEM companies in the U.S. market and an erosion of brand loyalty. Because of these consolidations, Ertl's vintage and Precision replicas have become even more important to its sales.

This Ertl MXU 285 is built in 1/32 scale and has a removable cab. It is a world-market toy of a world-market tractor.

Case IH had Ertl create a Collector's Edition of the big MX 285 to commemorate having built the 100,000th Maxxum series tractor.

Just as Case IH is an international company that builds and sells tractors all over the world, Ertl is an international toy company. Replicas of tractors that are sold in Europe as well as in the United States are often in 1/32 scale and have features, such as removable cabs, that European buyers demand.

To the delight of collectors, Ertl incorporated more detail into Collector and Special Edition tractors. The Collector Edition replicas had evolved from the days when they were barely distinguishable from shelf models to tractors with plastic windows in the cabs,

Case IH's Quadrac replaced the wheels of its articulated tractors with four-track units. This 1/16-scale replica is huge and weighs almost seven pounds.

The second Precision II toy, released in 2002, was this Case IH STX 450.

(middle left) This John Deere 5410 is aimed at the European market. It has a square, removable cab and was packed in a British package.

(middle right) John Deere had Ertl produce 2,500 of this 9300T replica at its Farm Show Special Edition in 2000. It has additional detail, railings, and other features not found on the shelf model.

(bottom left) The replica on the left is a Special Edition produced for John Deere's Waterloo plant employees in 2003. The shelf model is on the right.

(bottom right) The Collector's Edition John Deere 7920 features glass in the cab windows, authentic designs in the seat, and increased detail in the controls.

finely detailed interiors, and in some cases, the hoods opened to reveal highly detailed engines. Mirrors and lights that would never survive a season in the sandbox or might pose a hazard to a child could be added to these replicas because Ertl knew the tractors would never be used as toys. Tractors that were intended to be used as toys were plainer and designed with child safety in mind.

John Deere was aware of the success of Caterpillar's Challenger rubber-tracked tractor and produced a rubber track machine of its own in the late 1990s. The T tractors were large John Deere–wheeled tractors on an undercarriage designed for rubber treads. Deere wanted to promote the tractors and quickly had Ertl render them as toys. The first was a Model 8300T that was released as a 1/64-scale tractor in 1997. In 2000, a special 9300T-tracked tractor was created for the Farm Progress Show.

The Precision Classic John Deeres continued to be popular, and they became even more detailed. Ertl had created 14 Precision Classics and even a Special Edition

(opposite) These models of the Case IH MX 285 illustrate the differences between the shelf model (right) and the Collector's Edition.

(top left) In 2001 Ertl released its newest classic, the John Deere 4440 from 1978.

(top right) The photo of the rear of the 4440 Precision Classic shows the high level of detail. With a little dust and grease, it could pass for the real thing.

(bottom left) Priced at $105, the 9750 STS combine is a large model even in 1/32 scale.

(bottom right) The third replica in the Precision II series was this 9420T that was released in 2003.

(below left) Ertl's 1/64-scale toys fill a market niche between plastic toys built strictly for play, and its highly detailed replicas are intended for display.

(below right) While from the collector's viewpoint, the emphasis was on more precision and greater detail, Ertl did not forget the core of its business—building quality toys such as this Lego John Deere that can be assembled and disassembled.

Precision Classic for Deere. Interest in Precision Classic replicas showed no signs of abating as the new millennium dawned.

Ertl often teams with John Deere to produce a significant new product. John Deere was the first OEM to license Ertl, and it was also the first with 1/64-scale toys. John Deere was the first Collector Edition vintage tractor and the first Precision replica. So it was obvious that Ertl would choose John Deere for the first replica in two new series of replicas, Precision II and Prestige.

Ertl announced the Precision Series II toys in August 2001. Like Precision Classics, these were highly detailed toys, but they represented current production models in 1/32 scale. The first was the 2001 John Deere 9750 STS combine. The extraordinarily detailed replica was hand-assembled from more than 300 separate pieces. The cab door opens, the unloading auger moves, the cab ladder pivots, there are interchangeable corn and grain heads, and the rear panel opens.

That same year, Ertl and John Deere released a vintage Model 45 combine with a Number 10 corn head in the Prestige Series. Prestige replicas are 1/16 scale and more highly detailed than Collector Editions, but not so intricately appointed as Precision replicas. They use more plastic parts than a Precision replica, and somewhat less attention is paid to small details. Although they represent an excellent value, sales have been disappointing. Only one Prestige toy has been released in three years.

Ertl's Precision, Prestige, and Collector offerings had become so intricate they were no longer rated as toys. At the other end of the spectrum, Ertl is building toy tractors with a stronger emphasis on play value. These take a lot of imagination to be identified with the real thing, but they offer more interactive features than the classic diecast Ertl tractors. Between are dual-purpose 1/64- and 1/32-scale toys that have enough detail to satisfy adults but are safe and priced low enough to be given to children.

As Ertl approaches its 60th year, it has much to be proud of. From that first little red tractor cast in the basement of the Ertl family home, it has grown to an international toy-manufacturing phenomenon. Ertl persevered through the dark days of the OEM shakeups that began in the 1980s and found markets that no one had dreamed of in 1945. Its legacy of innovation and attention to detail continue to serve it well. There is little doubt that Ertl will still be making quality farm toys when it reaches its centennial year.

(above) This could be a scene right out of a mid-1960s hay field. The Precision Classic John Deere 3010 was released in 2001. The 314T baler was released in 1996.

(top left) At a retail price of less than $100, this Prestige Series John Deere 45 combine is an extraordinary value.

(top right) Sometimes you can mistake them for the real thing. This is the dashboard of the John Deere 3030 Precision Classic.

Glossary

Collector Edition—A collector edition is similar to a shelf model except there is usually a change in tooling, decals, paint scheme, or construction of the item. Collector editions will have diecast rims, three-point hitches, or other special features not found on the regular or shelf-model version. Collector editions will always have a diecast insert stating "Collector Edition." The packaging usually is marked as a collector edition as well.

Custom Edition—A toy replica made for special customers like the FFA, 4-H, or smaller toy shows. Modified shelf models are used and customized, usually with a decal and sometimes a diecast inscription.

Limited Edition—Farm-toy replicas that were made in specific, limited numbers. The number is set prior to accepting orders. Limited editions usually will have a decal, paint scheme, or construction change from other models made from the same tooling. Limited Edition, and sometimes "1 of xxxx" will appear on the toy, package, or both, but not always. This can be noted, but is not necessarily done, with a diecast insert or special decal.

OEM—Original Equipment Manufacturer. A company such as John Deere, International Harvester, or Ford that builds full-size tractors.

Precision Classics—Refers to the highly detailed John Deere farm-toy replicas first made by Ertl in 1990. Precision Classics have many more parts and greater detailing than most other farm toys. They are not made in any set limited quantities, but production is usually limited to two or three years.

Precision Series—The same as Precision Classics except they are replicas of makes other than John Deere.

Shelf/Regular Model—Replicas that are not limited in production. No inserts are diecast into the casting. These models usually have plastic rims and do not have detailing such as levers or three-point hitches. Length of production may vary from model to model. They are rated as toys.

Special Edition—Replicas that commemorate a special event such as new tractor introductions, dealer meetings, toy shows, and/or farm shows. The special event being commemorated may be listed on a diecast insert or on a decal. These may be a previously manufactured collector edition or shelf-model tractor with slight changes in the front axles or decaling.

Toy Rated—A replica that includes safety features that make it an appropriate toy.

Index